WITHDRAWN

Benjamin Banneker

Leaders of the Colonial Era

Lord Baltimore

Benjamin Banneker

William Bradford

Benjamin Franklin

Anne Hutchinson

Cotton Mather

William Penn

John Smith

Miles Standish

Peter Stuyvesant

3 1526 03967573 8

Leaders of the Colonial Era

Benjamin Banneker

Heather Lehr Wagner

BENJAMIN BANNEKER

Copyright © 2011 by Infobase Publishing

All rights reserved. No part of this book may be reproduced or utilized in any form or by any means, electronic or mechanical, including photocopying, recording, or by any information storage or retrieval systems, without permission in writing from the publisher. For information contact:

Chelsea House
An imprint of Infobase Publishing
132 West 31st Street
New York, NY 10001

Library of Congress Cataloging-in-Publication Data
Wagner, Heather Lehr.
  Benjamin Banneker / Heather Lehr Wagner.
    p. cm. — (Leaders of the colonial era)
  Includes bibliographical references and index.
  ISBN 978-1-60413-744-6 (hardcover)
 1. Banneker, Benjamin, 1731-1806. 2. Astronomers—United States—Biography. 3. African American scientists—Biography—Juvenile literature. 4. United States—History—Colonial period, ca. 1600-1775—Juvenile literature. I. Title. II. Series.
  QB36.B22W345 2010
  520.92—dc22
  [B]   2010009992

You can find Chelsea House on the World Wide Web at
http://www.chelseahouse.com.

Text design by Kerry Casey
Cover design by Keith Trego
Composition by EJB Publishing Services
Cover printed by Bang Printing, Brainerd, Minn.
Book printed and bound by Bang Printing, Brainerd, Minn.
Date printed: November 2010
Printed in the United States of America

10 9 8 7 6 5 4 3 2 1

This book is printed on acid-free paper.

All links and Web addresses were checked and verified to be correct at the time of publication. Because of the dynamic nature of the Web, some addresses and links may have changed since publication and may no longer be valid.

Contents

1	Building a Clock	7
2	Molly Welsh Arrives in America	17
3	A Boy in Maryland	30
4	Banneker the Farmer	40
5	Studying the Stars	51
6	Surveying a New Capital	61
7	Almanac Author	75
8	Final Years	85

Chronology and Timeline	92
Bibliography	95
Further Resources	97
Picture Credits	98
Index	99
About the Author	102

1

Building a Clock

For teenage Benjamin Banneker, the responsibility of helping his father run the family farm meant that he had little time for the things that interested him. In colonial Maryland, where Benjamin lived, tobacco—the farm's chief crop—was a vital export, and it operated on a strict cycle.

In the spring, the seeds from the previous year's plants were sowed in special seedbeds covered with ash. On the Banneky (as the family was then known) farm, these seedbeds were close to the woods, where the soil was especially rich and where young plants could take root shielded from the heat of the sun. The location, next to the woods, meant that the spring planting had to be carefully watched to ensure that wild animals did not dig up the seeds and eat them.

Once the tobacco plants sent out their shoots, usually after about a month, each plant had to be carefully dug up, surrounded by enough soil to avoid damaging the roots, and then carried to the tobacco field and replanted. This could only be done when it was raining or had rained recently, so that the ground would be soft. Once more Benjamin needed to guard the plants, this time to protect them from insects that might ruin the crop by eating the plants or from the weeds that could choke them. Every day (except Sunday, the one day that the family rested) Benjamin, his parents, and his three younger sisters went out into the fields to pick off any slugs, aphids, caterpillars, or worms that might have crawled onto the plants. Using hoes or their bare hands, they pulled out any weeds. After the plant had sprouted between 10 and 15 leaves, its top had to be cut off to prevent it from growing too tall and to keep the leaves strong. Any suckers that the plant sent out then had to be gently pulled off.

Next, as the plants began to flower, the best and strongest would be selected for use as seed plants to guarantee future harvests. These were covered with small cloth bags, which needed to be checked and adjusted as the flower beneath began to grow. When the flower became partially dried, the seeds needed to be cut off and hung to dry, before the seeds were shelled and set aside for next year's planting. Weather made the whole process uncertain—too much rain or too dry a summer could bring disaster for the crop.

By August, as the summer heat beat down on their central Maryland farm, Benjamin and his family needed to prepare the tobacco crop for harvest. The large leaves of tobacco needed to be cut from the plant, gathered from the field, and carried to a special building on the farm called a "tobacco house." There, the leaves were hung up and dried for five or six weeks, a process known as curing.

In mid-eighteenth century Maryland, tobacco was the colony's chief crop, and most farms specialized in tobacco. Generally these

Building a Clock 9

Farmworkers harvest tobacco leaves on a Virginia plantation in the 1600s. Benjamin Banneker did the same work on his family's Maryland farm. Tobacco was a highly prized export for the colonies to ship to England.

were large plantations using slave labor. But many smaller family farms, like the Bannekys' farm, also produced tobacco. There was a strong demand for tobacco in Britain and the rest of Europe, and the laws governing its production and marketing were strict. Tobacco had to be taken to market in a special bundle known as a hogshead. According to Maryland law, this hogshead had to be a specific size: 48 inches (122 centimeters) high and 32 inches (81.3 cm) wide.

After the tobacco leaves had hung for five or six weeks, they were dry but still flexible enough to be shaped into hogsheads. Benjamin and his family took the leaves down and then pushed and prodded the leaves tightly together into the proper shape so that they would fit into the hogsheads that had been bought from a cooper at one of

A LETTER TO THOMAS JEFFERSON

On August 19, 1791, Benjamin Banneker wrote to Thomas Jefferson, then serving as the country's first secretary of state, contrasting Jefferson's phrase, "We hold these truths to be self-evident, that all men are created equal," written for the Declaration of Independence, with the discrimination against people of color in the new country. This excerpt comes from that letter:

> I suppose it is a truth too well attested to you, to need a proof here, that we are a race of beings who have long laboured under the abuse and censure of the world, that we have long been considered rather as brutish than human, and scarcely capable of mental endowments.
>
> Sir, I hope I may safely admit, in consequence of that report which hath reached me, that you are a man far less inflexible in sentiments of this nature than many others, that you are measureably friendly and well disposed towards us, and that you are ready and willing to lend your aid and assistance to our relief, from those many distressed and numerous calamities, to which we are reduced.
>
> Now, sir, if this is founded in truth, I apprehend you will readily embrace every opportunity to eradicate that train of absurd and false ideas and opinions, which so generally prevails with respect to us, and that your sentiments are concurrent with mine, which are that one universal father hath given being to us all, and that he hath not only made

the nearby river towns. The hogsheads were then rolled to markets, pulled either by horses or oxen, along roads constructed specifically for this purpose, known as rolling roads. The rolling roads connected us all of one flesh, but that he hath also without partiality afforded us all the same sensations, and endued us all with the same faculties, and that however variable we may be in society or religion, however diversified in situation or colour, we are all of the same family, and stand in the same relation to him.

Sir, if these are sentiments of which you are fully persuaded, I hope you cannot but acknowledge, that it is the indispensable duty of those who maintain for themselves the rights of human nature, and who profess the obligations of Christianity, to extend their power and influence to the relief of every part of the human race, from whatever burthen or oppression they may unjustly labour under, and this I apprehend a full conviction of the truth and obligation of these principles should lead all to.

Sir, I have long been convinced, that if your love for yourselves and for those inestimable laws, which preserve to you the rights of human nature, was founded on sincerity, you could not but be solicitous that every individual of whatever rank or distinction, might with you equally enjoy the blessings thereof, neither could you rest satisfied, short of the most active diffusion of your exertions, in order, to their promotion from any state of degradation, to which the unjustifiable cruelty and barbarism of men may have reduced them.

[Quoted in Herb Boyd, *Autobiography of a People: Three Centuries of African American History Told by Those Who Lived It* (New York: Doubleday, 2000), pp. 52–53.]

farms throughout the region with the docks at the Patapsco River. There, they would be sold to a tobacco broker, who could ship the tobacco to England. Payment for the hogsheads came not in pounds

(Maryland was still a British colony) but in what were called "tobacco notes," notes that specified the weight of the tobacco sold, the type of tobacco leaf, and the name of the warehouse that had purchased it. These tobacco notes served as a kind of money throughout colonial Maryland; they could be used to pay taxes or fees, to buy land, or to purchase goods and supplies.

For young Benjamin the cycle of tobacco marked his teenage life. He once counted 36 separate steps involved in each tobacco crop, and helping with the tobacco was not his only responsibility on the farm. The family also grew corn and wheat for their own use, and these too had to be planted, weeded, and cared for until they were harvested. Tobacco was very hard on soil, and so the tobacco fields had to be rotated and the soil nourished again. This was done by what was called "cowpenning," moving the cows from one planting area to another and then setting up portable fences to keep them in place. The cow manure would help nourish the soil. Benjamin was responsible for the cowpenning, and he also went with his father by wagon to the marshes near the Patapsco River to shovel some of the rich marsh soil into the wagon. This marsh soil was taken back to the farm and spread out to dry, checked for roots and rocks (which needed to be removed), and then used to help provide the soil for a new crop of tobacco.

The family had only a few animals—some cows, two horses, a few pigs and chickens—but these all needed to be cared for and fed. In winter, Benjamin helped his father cut trees to provide firewood for the farm and went with him to hunt and trap.

Often colonial farmers would band together to help harvest crops or raise barns. But the Banneky family did not benefit from this community support. In a colony where much of the tobacco farming was performed by slave labor, the Bannekys were quite unusual. They were black, and they were free.

STUDYING TIME

Many of the farmers who lived in the surrounding communities were suspicious of the Bannekys, worried that the presence of free blacks might inspire their slaves to rebel and attempt to win their own freedom. Free blacks in eighteenth-century Maryland were social outcasts, unable to find a place in the community either with their white neighbors or slaves. The Bannekys had no desire to antagonize anyone. They had deliberately purchased 100 acres (40.5 hectares) of farmland in a remote part of central Maryland, on the southern side of the Patapsco River in Baltimore County. Their nearest neighbor was Benjamin's grandmother.

They kept to themselves, and the remote location of the farm, plus the demands of farm life, meant that Benjamin spent little time with anyone except his family. He had briefly attended a country school for a few winters as a boy, but once he was old enough to work full time on the farm he was needed by his father.

But Benjamin possessed a curious, active mind. He had been taught to read and write by his grandmother, and he had learned basic arithmetic during his brief time in school. He had no books of his own as a young man, but he took advantage of the world around him to continue to learn. He studied the nature and wildlife around the farm. He was fascinated by mechanics and mastered the use and repair of the tools needed to run the farm.

By the time Benjamin was nearly 20, his path seemed clear. He would help his father run the family farm and, eventually, run it himself. He would spend his time with family members who admired his curiosity but did not share his deep interest in learning new skills.

Then came an event that dramatically changed Benjamin's life. And it all began with a pocket watch. Watches and clocks were a luxury and quite rare in eighteenth-century America. Those that existed

14 BENJAMIN BANNEKER

Although Benjamin Banneker was a free black in colonial America, he and his family did not have a place in society. Thus, he spent a lot of time on his own, feeding his curious mind and learning about the things around him.

were often family heirlooms, treasured items that had been brought over from Europe.

There was not the same need to keep constant track of time in the colonial period. Farmers relied on the rising and setting of the sun to mark the beginning and end of their workday. In the more populous towns, church bells could be heard ringing the hours, but for colonists living on farms and plantations well outside of town, there were no church bells to mark the passage of time.

Despite the rarity of clocks and pocket watches, when he was about 20 years old, Benjamin somehow met someone with a pocket watch and was able to study it closely. Dick Russell, writing in *Black Genius and the American Experience*, suggests that it happened when Benjamin had taken the family's tobacco crop to market on the coast. There, according to Russell, he met a traveling salesman named Josef Levi who showed Benjamin his pocket watch and then allowed him to borrow it for a few days.

Whether it was the pocket watch of a traveling salesman or a merchant or another farmer, it is certain that Benjamin met someone with a pocket watch who was willing to lend it to him for a few days. Benjamin then carefully took apart the watch, studying and making drawings of its parts. He inspected each piece, noting how the wheels that marked the seconds, minutes, and hours meshed. He studied each component of the pocket watch, then reassembled it and returned it to its owner in perfect working condition.

For the next two years, whenever he had a free minute, he thought about the watch. He studied his drawings of the watch's components, first considering the wheels. He counted the number of teeth of each wheel and studied their size. He then decided to make models of the wheels, carving and polishing pieces of wood into the correct shape, using a small knife to carefully whittle each tooth in the proper way so that, eventually, the wooden wheels would mesh together as perfectly as those of the watch had. They were far larger than the wheels of the pocket watch, but they were otherwise a perfect match.

Gradually, he turned his attention to the other components of the watch, carving and shaping them out of wood just as he had done with the wheels. He used a few bits of iron and brass when needed, but for the most part he worked entirely with wood. He added a framework and a dial and finally a bell.

At the end, Benjamin had built a clock, a working clock that chimed on the hour. Simply by studying the parts of a pocket watch for a few days, and without any additional training, Benjamin had accomplished a task that only the most skilled eighteenth-century craftsmen could master: building a working clock. The clock kept accurate time for more than 40 years.

The building of this clock was the first sign that Benjamin Banneker was not destined for an ordinary life. Neighboring farmers and merchants, when they learned of the accomplishment, would travel to the family farm to see the clock that Benjamin had built. And long after he had done other, more impressive things, people would still remember that Benjamin Banneker once built a wooden clock that kept perfect time.

2
Molly Welsh Arrives in America

The story of Benjamin Banneker begins when a young, white servant girl from England, Molly Welsh, arrived in America. Molly had worked in England for a cattle farmer, and one of her responsibilities was milking the cows. One day a cow kicked over a pail of milk. When Molly tried to tell her employer what had happened, he refused to believe her. Instead, he accused Molly of stealing the milk.

The penalty for stealing was strict in seventeenth-century England. Someone found guilty of stealing could be sentenced to death by hanging. Molly was saved from this fate by one simple skill: Molly knew how to read.

In the English judicial system of the time, a prisoner convicted of a felony could "call for the book." When a book was produced, the prisoner had to prove that he or she could read it. If he could, his thumb was branded or he could choose to be pardoned on the condition that he leave the country. He would be transported overseas to work as a servant for seven years.

The goal of this system was, in part, to supply desperately needed labor to the American colonies. In the seventeenth century, there was a great demand for workers to help run the plantations that were springing up in the colonies. It would not be until the beginning of the eighteenth century that enslaved Africans would replace European servants as the main source of forced labor in the American colonies. This system provided many financial rewards for those involved in transporting forced labor. The sheriffs in England would arrange to transport exiled convicts with ship merchants dealing with plantation owners in the colonies. The merchants would then pay for a bond as a guarantee of the safe transportation of the human cargo. The sheriffs and the merchants were both paid for their part in providing the labor. Finally, the plantation owner received free labor from the convict for seven years.

It was a difficult and frightening journey across the Atlantic Ocean for Molly Welsh. Her exact age at the time of the crossing is unknown, but when she later recounted her life story to her grandson, Benjamin Banneker, she said that she had still been a girl at the time, probably in her teens. As many as 150 to 200 convicts would be crowded onto a small ship. It was not uncommon for many of these convicts to be younger than 12 years old. Depending on the weather, the journey could last anywhere from 47 to 138 days, according to Silvio Bedini in *The Life of Benjamin Banneker*. Because it was difficult to predict exactly how long the voyage would last, food and water often ran out before the ship had arrived in port in Maryland or Virginia. Molly would have been given a weekly allowance of bread, cheese, butter, and some salted meat (usually pork), as well as some peas.

SEVEN YEARS PASSENGERS

In the seventeenth and eighteenth centuries, convicted felons from England were transported to the American colonies (the majority to Maryland) to provide forced labor for a period generally lasting seven years. For this reason, they were often called "seven years passengers" when a ship announced their arrival in the local newspapers. There was a great demand for laborers on plantations and in the cities of colonial America, and shipowners would provide transportation at their own expense for convicts and impoverished workers seeking jobs in the colonies. They would receive any costs back plus a profit when the workers were sold.

Farmworkers and house servants, carpenters, masons, mechanics, even clerks and teachers (who served as private tutors to the children of wealthy families) were all desperately needed in the colonies. The employers were responsible for providing food, clothing, and shelter for their servants. After their period of service had ended, the servants were eligible to purchase land and establish an independent life in their new home.

Silvio Bedini in *The Life of Benjamin Banneker* quotes a notice from *The Maryland Gazette* of November 24, 1768, announcing the arrival of a shipment of servants:

> Just imported from Bristol, in the Ship Randolph, Capt. John Weber Price, One Hundred and Fifteen Convicts, men, women, and lads: Among whom are several Tradesmen, who are to be sold on board the said Ship, now in Annapolis Dock, this Day, Tomorrow, and Saturday next, by Smyth & Sudler.

When the ships finally arrived in port, in Molly's case along the Chesapeake Bay of Maryland, they sailed up and down the river, posting notices in the local newspapers that their cargo included servants or what, at the time, were called "seven years passengers."

A PERIOD OF SERVICE

It was around 1683 that Molly Welsh first arrived in Maryland, on board an English ship that docked either at Londontown or Providence (a city now known as Annapolis). She was then sold, the price paid for her being used to help cover the cost of her transportation to America. Her new employer was a tobacco farmer who had a plantation on the Patapsco River.

For the next seven years, Molly worked for her master from dawn to dusk. She had been a servant in England, so she was accustomed to hard work. Her master gave her clothing, shelter, and food. She was required to be obedient, to perform whatever tasks her master ordered her to perform, and strictly forbidden to steal. Masters were entitled to beat servants who disobeyed them in any way. Servants were not allowed to go any farther than 10 miles (16.1 kilometers) from their master's property without a special written pass. The conditions were difficult and the treatment was often harsh, but servants like Molly (known as indentured servants) were better off than the African slaves later brought in to work on plantations. Indentured servants worked for a specific period of time, at the end of which they were free.

Molly's employer treated her fairly. She probably worked in the fields of his plantation, rather than the house, as she later had the knowledge and skills to set up her own tobacco farm.

Around 1690, Molly Welsh finally won her freedom. She was in her mid-20s, blond and fair-skinned, and determined to build a life for herself in the colonies rather than trying to earn enough to pay for transportation back to England. She found a small plot of farmland for rent, about 12 miles (19.3 km) from the Patapsco River. The rent could be paid in tobacco.

Molly made arrangements to rent the farm and set to work using the farming knowledge she had gathered when she was a servant. The farm was in the middle of a wilderness, and Molly—working alone—had to clear the trees and plant corn and tobacco. She was hardworking and ambitious, and for several years she had successful harvests, earning enough from the sale of tobacco not only to pay her rent but to put a little money aside. After several years, she was able to purchase land of her own, most likely the farm she had been renting.

LANDOWNER AND EMPLOYER

By 1692, Molly Welsh's farm had grown to the point where she could no longer work the land on her own. She needed help, but she could not afford to pay the fees to hire local workers or even indentured servants as she had been.

When she had taken her tobacco crop to market in the nearby river towns, she had seen English ships arriving with their cargo of African slaves. Those slaves who seemed the strongest were sold quickly and at prices beyond what Molly could afford. She had mixed feelings about slavery after her own experience as a forced laborer. Other slave agents brought slaves along the "rolling roads" that wound from the port to the tobacco farms far from the coast. They hoped to sell the slaves that had not sold at auction at reduced prices to farmers in need of labor. These slaves were often ill or weak, and Molly refused to pay for these hopeless-looking men and women.

Finally, as the pressure of trying to maintain her farm increased, Molly decided to purchase two slaves when she took her tobacco crop to sell at the end of the summer. Prices for slaves were often lower at the end of the summer, once the tobacco crops had been harvested, than they were in the early spring.

22 BENJAMIN BANNEKER

This illustration shows a public slave auction in the United States. Those who didn't sell at auction were peddled inland by agents. Although she was hesitant to do so, Molly Welsh decided to purchase two such slaves to help her tend her growing farm.

Molly studied the slaves and selected two young men from Africa. One was strong and very healthy. The other seemed far thinner and less likely to be a hard worker, but his price was low and there was something about him that appealed to Molly.

Her instincts proved correct. The first slave—whose name is not known—was a hard worker who quickly proved an invaluable assistant in the heavy labor involved in tobacco farming. He helped Molly clear trees to open up new stretches of land for farming. He helped build a new shed for curing the tobacco. He helped plow the fields and later harvested the crops.

As Molly had suspected, the other slave was weaker and less willing to work. Molly gave him some of the lighter chores involved in running the farm, and gradually she was able to communicate with him. He told her that his name was Bannaka or Bannka. He said that he was the son of an African chief and told Molly that he had been captured by slave traders, thrown onto a slave ship, and transported to the American colonies against his will.

Molly was impressed by Bannaka's stories of his life as an "African prince," as Molly later told her grandson. She excused his unwillingness to perform any labor on the farm as understandable, given his background, and she admired his intelligence, his good manners, and his thoughtful personality. Gradually, the hardworking man decided to convert to Molly's faith of Christianity, but Bannaka (gradually called "Banneky") remained firmly tied to the beliefs and practices that had defined his life in Africa.

After several years, Molly decided to give both servants their freedom, an unusual act in Maryland at that time. Soon after that, Molly decided on an even more unusual—and dangerous—act. She decided to marry Banneky.

INTERRACIAL MARRIAGE

Molly Welsh's decision to marry her former slave was made knowing that such a marriage in colonial Maryland was against the law. In *Blacks in Colonial America*, author Oscar Reiss notes that in 1661 in Maryland, a white woman who married a black slave became the servant of his owner during his lifetime, and her children would also be slaves. By 1681, free whites (male or female) in Maryland found to be married to a black person would become an indentured servant for seven years, their black spouse would be enslaved for life, and their children would be forced to serve for 31 years.

Maryland was not the only colony to ban interracial marriage. Many of the colonies passed separate laws and enacted fines for those involved and their children. Massachusetts made interracial marriage illegal in 1705. Pennsylvania did the same in 1725, and it added a heavy fine for ministers who performed interracial marriage ceremonies.

Molly Welsh faced the loss of her freedom, the loss of her farm, and all that she had worked so hard to achieve. She could not have made the decision to marry Banneky without knowing the risks, and she spent the rest of her life aware that her choices, her husband's status, and the biracial children they would later have all faced dangers simply because of who they were. The problem was further complicated by the fact that there was no proof that she, or her husband, was free. No documents had been provided to Molly when her term of service ended. She had given her slaves their freedom orally, without any formal documents being filed. Lacking these documents, her husband could be seized at any time and face the prospect of being sold back into slavery. Molly's solution was to retreat from any interaction with the white farmers who lived nearby, a relatively easy task given the remote location of her small farm in the wilderness of Maryland. She took her husband's name, and eventually they had four daughters.

Their oldest daughter, Mary, was born in 1700. From a young age she helped her mother work the farm, learning to plant and harvest the tobacco that provided their livelihood.

A QUIET LIFE

While the Banneky family worked their farm and lived a life separate from other colonial farmers, the region around the Patapsco River was growing in population. There was increasing demand for tobacco, and the area along the Patapsco was known to be a fertile territory for the plant's cultivation. In 1707, the settlement of Joppa was established at a point where several of the "rolling roads" used to transport the tobacco to the port towns converged. Joppa became the county seat in 1712 and eventually a center for tobacco trade.

While Molly's daughters were still young, Banneky died after an illness. He had never fully adapted to the cold winters of Maryland, and diseases (including yellow fever) claimed many lives in that part of the colonies. The exact year of his death, and its cause, are not known. Molly was left with four young daughters to raise and a farm to manage.

Her oldest daughter, Mary, was a source of strength and support. Silvio Bedini notes that she was later described as a very intelligent woman, expert in the use of herbs, attractive and tall with long black hair that never became gray. She helped raise her sisters and worked on her mother's farm for many years, waiting to marry until she was nearly 30 years old. Her husband was a man from Guinea, Africa, who had been kidnapped by slave traders and sold into slavery, eventually working for a tobacco planter who lived near the Bannekys. He had been given the name Robert when he converted to Christianity and was baptized. Soon after, he had been freed.

Robert and Mary were married soon after he won his freedom. Because he did not have a last name, he took his wife's name and became Robert Banneky.

The couple lived with Molly at first, helping her to work the farm and receiving a share of the profits, which they saved to buy their own farm. One by one, Molly's other daughters married and moved away from home, but Mary and Robert remained, helping with the farm and slowly producing a new generation that became a part of the Banneky life. Their first child was a son, born on November 9, 1731. They called him Benjamin.

A FARM OF THEIR OWN

It took several years for Mary and Robert to save enough money to purchase their own land. Finally, they had enough for a small stretch of land—some 25 acres (10.1 ha)—near Molly's farm. The area was east of the Patapsco Falls, in Baltimore County, and was heavily wooded. Its name, appropriately, was Timber Poynt.

The heavy woods were a challenge for someone interested in farming, but Robert and Mary had worked hard to save enough for their farm, and they spent several months clearing the land and planting tobacco, corn, and wheat. They planted a small vegetable garden and a few fruit trees to provide their family with food. In addition to the work of running their own farm, Robert and Mary also helped Molly with hers. The family continued to live with Molly.

For Robert, the small stretch of land was only the beginning. He continued to diligently save as much of the profit from his tobacco as possible, in the hopes of expanding his farm. There was a stretch of land he had dreamed of owning, land that he had seen as he worked at Molly's farm. It was a short distance from hers and consisted of 100 acres (40.5 ha), once part of a larger plantation. The land was fertile and had a stream nearby, useful for helping to irrigate the crops.

Finally, Robert had saved enough for the land. The price was 7,000 pounds of tobacco. The deed to the land was drawn up on March 10, 1737, giving the 100 acres jointly to Robert Banneky and his son, Benjamin. Robert had this wording inserted into the document specifically, to ensure that nothing could prevent his son from inheriting that land upon Robert's death. Freedom and the right to own land were precious things that neither Robert nor Mary took for granted, and they wanted to ensure that their son would be able to continue to benefit from their hard-won freedom long after they had gone.

> Head Quarters Department of the South,
> Port Royal, S.C. August 22nd 1862.
>
> Agreeably to the laws of the United States of America, the bearer, London Henry, once claimed as a Slave, is declared forever free. Wives, Mothers, and Children, of all those declared free, are also forever free:
>
> D. Hunter,
> Major General Commanding.

Free blacks were only somewhat "free" during Banneker's younger days in colonial Maryland. They did not share the rights of white men, and they were required to carry their Certificate of Freedom at all times. An example of such a document—Henry London's free papers—is shown above.

Every bit of Robert and Mary's savings was spent to purchase the farm, and so the first years were challenging. It is likely that they lived with Molly until Robert could clear two areas of land on his new farm. The priority was given to clearing the area where tobacco would be planted. After that, he could clear the land where the family home would be built.

Clearing the land was challenging work. First the underbrush had to be cleared out and any larger roots pulled up out of the soil. Trees had to be cut down and dried. The trees all had to be cut down so that they fell in one direction. They would form furrows in the ground, which later Robert would follow to ease the task of plowing. There was not enough time to pull out all the tree stumps. Eventually, they decayed.

Robert quickly planted corn and tobacco and then, as spring gave way to summer, he began to build a house. The best tree trunks he had cleared from the farmland were taken to a sawmill up the river and made into logs and boards, which could then be used to build his house. Everyone helped with the farmwork and construction, even five-year-old Benjamin. Their focus was on the tobacco crop. Once it had been harvested, taken to market and sold in the fall, they could continue to work on building their home.

In eighteenth-century America it was common for neighboring farmers to band together to help with harvesting crops and building homes. But the Bannekys were on their own. There was an increasing amount of prejudice against free blacks, particularly among farmers who were slave owners, and most free blacks lived as outcasts.

FREEDOM IN MARYLAND

By the eighteenth century, slavery had spread throughout most of colonial America. But the largest employers of African slaves were the colonies along the Chesapeake specializing in tobacco plantations—Virginia and Maryland—as well as the rice plantations in South Carolina and Georgia. The demand for labor on the tobacco plantations was great—it was this that had brought Molly Welsh and other indentured servants to the region—and in the 1650s, this labor force changed from white servants from Europe to black slaves. From 1670 to 1720, thousands of African slaves were brought into the Chesapeake region. According to Michael L. Conniff and Thomas J. Davis's *Africans in the Americas*, by 1750 blacks made up more than 30 percent of Maryland's population.

There were four ways in which blacks could be freed in the late seventeenth century: They could buy their own freedom; someone could buy their freedom for them; they could earn their freedom through hard work and faithful service; they could be born to non-slave mothers. As Michael Conniff and Thomas Davis note in *Africans in the Americas*, most blacks were slaves and those who were free were rarely prosperous. By the mid-1700s, there were fewer and fewer free blacks, and the number who owned land was very small. Divisions between whites and blacks sharpened.

From 1752 to 1772, it was illegal to free a slave in Maryland. Freed slaves were required to carry a "Certificate of Freedom," which stated their name, age, physical characteristics, and the name of their former owner. Free blacks could not vote, sue whites, or testify against them in court. They were prohibited from holding certain jobs and could be sold back into slavery if they entered Maryland from another colony or could not pay taxes or fines owed.

Because the laws governing their status were so challenging, and because the prejudice against free blacks was growing in Maryland, the Banneky family kept largely to themselves. They relied on their own strength and hard work to carve out a living.

3

A Boy in Maryland

The home Robert Banneky built for his family was a one-room log cabin with a loft, built from the trees he had cut down himself. There were openings in the walls for windows, but glass was too expensive for the Banneky family. Instead, Robert built heavy wooden shutters and attached them to the inside, so that the shutters could be closed in cold weather. The floor was also made of logs—logs split in half and smoothed. The fireplace filled nearly one side of the one-room house. It was made of stones that had been cleared from the farmland, held in place with clay and moss.

Benjamin Banneker grew up in a home his father had built whose only furniture was the simple pieces his father had made by hand. There was a table—really a large slab of wood—into which holes had been drilled and legs inserted. Each member of the family (including

Benjamin, his parents, and his three younger sisters—Jemima, Minta, and Molly) had his or her own wooden stool. Beds were made of wooden slabs placed across wooden poles held up by wooden posts. The home was heated by firewood, and it was lit at night by burning pine knots. His mother cooked using an iron pot and iron fork. Most of her other utensils were made from gourds grown on the farm.

The food they ate was also largely the result of what they grew or caught themselves. They ate game—rabbits, geese, ducks, squirrels, deer, wild turkeys, opossums, and raccoons that first Robert, and later Benjamin, hunted—as well as fish from the nearby river. They ate corn bread, eggs, milk, and chicken from their farm and whatever vegetables they could harvest in the summer and fall. Dried corn provided another staple—hominy (a kind of oatmeal made from corn). After several years, the fruit trees Robert planted began to produce pears, plums, and apples. There were beehives, from which Benjamin learned to collect honey.

Benjamin's mother, Mary, was known for her knowledge of herbs, and she was an expert in their use in healing minor aches and ailments. Certain plants could be brewed to make teas that would soothe a sore throat or an upset stomach. Others healed cuts or reduced swelling. Mary made her own candles from bayberries. She raised flax, hemp, and cotton plants to make clothing. She made brooms from the reeds that grew along the river.

There was constant work on the farm. The Bannekys, because of their status as free blacks, would have found it difficult to hire workers. Many free blacks chose to purchase slaves to work their farms, but the Bannekys did not.

EARLY EDUCATION

Benjamin was kept busy at the farm, but the little free time he had was spent at his grandmother's farm. The ability to read had kept her

Benjamin Banneker grew up simply, in a house built by his father, with very few furnishings. Banneker spent most of his time outdoors working or exploring, or indoors studying the Bible.

alive, and she was determined that her grandson would have the same skill. She taught Benjamin to read and write and also focused on his religious education. On Sundays, when there were no farm chores to be done, Benjamin's grandmother pulled out the large Bible she had ordered from England and asked him to read to her. Soon Benjamin was memorizing passages, astonishing her with his quick mind and impressing her with his eagerness to learn.

Molly taught Benjamin his numbers, encouraging him to count trees, birds, and anything else he could find. Finally, when she had taught him everything she knew, she arranged for him to attend a small school that had recently opened near her farm. It was a one-room school with a single teacher, which operated only during the winter months when the children were not needed to help in the fields. There were only a few students—some white and a few (like Benjamin) the children of free blacks.

Benjamin soon became friends with Jacob Hall, whose father had been a slave who had won his freedom and 13 acres (5.3 ha) of land in Baltimore County from a grateful master. Hall would become a lifelong friend. He later noted (as quoted in *The Life of Benjamin Banneker*) that, even as a boy, Benjamin had not spent a lot of time playing but, instead "all his delight was to dive into his books."

Benjamin spent only a few months each year in school, and when he was old enough to work all day with his father, he no longer attended. But the brief period made a deep impression on him, sparking a lifelong love of learning and a passion for math. His familiarity with advanced math, for example, suggests that he was able to borrow books (perhaps from his former teacher) in order to continue to learn on his own.

THE THREAT

The Banneky family, like many who belonged to the small population of free blacks in Maryland, lived quietly, far removed from their neighbors. This isolation provided Benjamin with a certain amount of ignorance of the threat of enslavement that faced people of color when he was very young, but an incident when he was with his grandmother gave him a far greater understanding of his status in Maryland in that time before the Revolutionary War.

As described by Charles Cerami in his biography of Banneker, the incident took place when Benjamin was a boy. He and several of his cousins had gone with his grandmother, Molly, to a fair in

> ## OLAUDAH EQUIANO
>
> The horrors of slavery haunted many people of color living in colonial America. The experiences of Olaudah Equiano illustrate the terrors of bondage. Equiano was born in the region of Africa now known as Nigeria. At the age of 11 he was kidnapped by members of a hostile tribe and transported on a British slave ship to the New World, where he became a servant to British naval officers serving in the colonies. He finally purchased his freedom from a Quaker merchant in 1766. His autobiography, *The Interesting Narrative of the Life of Olaudah Equiano, or Gustavus Vassa, the African*, was published in 1789. In this excerpt, he describes the horror of being sold at a slave auction:
>
> > We were not many days in the merchants' custody before we were sold after the usual manner, which is this: On a signal given, such as the beat of a drum, the buyers rush at once into the yard where the slaves are confined, and make choice of that parcel they like best. The noise and clamour with which this is attended, and the eagerness visible in the countenances of the buyers, serve not a little to increase the apprehensions of the terrified Africans, who may well be supposed to consider them the ministers of

the nearby port town of Elkridge Landing. The children had wandered away from their grandmother to admire something, when they were suddenly surrounded by four burly white men, who harshly demanded, "Who do you belong to?" The frightened children did not know how to respond until Molly hurried over. Drawing herself up, she moved between the children and the men and loudly announced

> that destruction to which they think themselves devoted. In this manner, without scruple, are relations and friends separated, most of them never to see each other again. I remember in the vessel in which I was brought over in, in the man's apartment, there were several brothers, who, in the sale, were sold in different lots; and it was very moving on this occasion to see their distress and hear their cries at parting. . . . Is it not enough that we are torn from our country and friends, to toil for your luxury and lust of gain? Must every tender feeling be likewise sacrificed to your avarice? Are the dearest friends and relations now rendered more dear by their separation from the rest of their kindred, still to be parted from each other, and thus prevented from cheering the gloom of slavery, with the small comfort of being together, and mingling their sufferings and sorrows? Why are parents to lose their children, brothers their sisters, or husbands their wives? Surely this is a new refinement in cruelty, which, while it has no advantage to atone for it, thus aggravates distress, and adds fresh horrors even to the wretchedness of slavery.
>
> [Excerpted in Deirdre Mullane (ed.), *Crossing the Danger Water: Three Hundred Years of African-American Writing* (New York: Doubleday, 1993), p. 19.]

that these were "my slaves' children, of course." The men murmured their apologies and moved off.

According to Cerami, this incident haunted Benjamin well into adulthood. It pointed out several facts that he had not previously encountered in his sheltered childhood. There was a clear difference between the races—white children could freely roam the fair without question, while black children were only permissible if they "belonged" to someone else. His safety was no longer certain—he now understood a bit better why his family lived so far from their neighbors and kept to themselves. Even his beloved grandmother could not acknowledge their relationship when threatened; instead their safety depended on her pretending to own slaves, pretending that Benjamin and his cousins were her property.

HARD WORK

As he grew older, Benjamin worked side by side with his father. Their focus was on the precious tobacco crop. It constantly demanded attention and as the dominant crop in the region provided the main source of income not only for the Bannekys but for most of those living in Maryland and Virginia. A letter written in 1729 by Leonard Calvert, the royal governor of Maryland, and quoted in Frederick Gutheim's *The Potomac*, notes: "In Virginia and Maryland Tobacco is our staple, is our All, and indeed leaves no room for anything Else; It requires the Attendance of all our hands, and Exacts their utmost labour, the whole year around."

Throughout Maryland there were both large plantations and small farms like the Bannekys', all busily engaged in the process of growing and harvesting tobacco. It was grueling labor, requiring all members of the family to help with its many stages. Unlike rice or cotton, it required year-round attention, from protecting the tiny seeds through the winter to the final transporting of the large barrels of tobacco to market in late fall.

Benjamin was expected to help with each stage of the process. From early in the spring until summer, this meant planting, weeding, and picking insects off the plants. In August, he helped cut the tobacco leaves and carry them to the tobacco house, where they

A Boy in Maryland 37

Tobacco farms were especially grueling to maintain—the work was year-round. After harvesting and preparing the crop, Benjamin and his family would transport the tobacco to an agent for an English merchant.

would be hung to dry. After a month of drying, or "curing," the leaves had to be taken down and the stalks removed. This had to be done while the leaves were still moist enough to be handled without breaking. They were then packed tightly into bundles and pushed into barrels, or hogsheads, and moved along the rolling roads to the tobacco market, where they could be sold.

Larger tobacco plantations in the region dealt with a London merchant, who arranged for the marketing and transportation of their tobacco, but the Bannekys sold their tobacco directly to an agent for an English merchant at the river landing. They were paid in tobacco notes; the agent then shipped their tobacco directly to England. They could then use their tobacco notes to buy goods in town or pay bills or taxes.

In addition to assisting with the tobacco crop, Benjamin was also responsible for helping with the family's other crops—corn, wheat, oats, rye, barley, flax, beans, cabbage, potatoes, onions, and squash. He gathered fruit from the family's orchard and helped his father hunt and trap game and fish. He was responsible for moving the family's six cows from one portion of the farm to another to fertilize different patches of land. He helped care for three pigs, two horses, and a small flock of chickens.

It was an increasingly isolated life, as Benjamin left school and spent more time on the family farm. He challenged his mind by applying mathematical principles to his chores, determining that the process of cultivating tobacco took 36 separate steps. He explored the forests and fields nearby, as well as the Patapsco River that flowed about a mile from his home, studying nature and noting differences among the birds and animals that populated the region.

There were few accesses to news when Benjamin was young. There were no newspapers published in Maryland until Benjamin was about 14 years old, when the *Maryland Gazette* began printing. The Bannekys would seldom have seen it in their remote location, nor would it have been of great interest to them. There was little news in its early editions; instead, its focus was on the arrivals and departures of ships, advertisements of cargo, and notices of runaway slaves.

Instead, the family gathered news periodically from the rare craftsmen who passed by their farm. Cobblers, blacksmiths, and tailors traveled about the region using a horse and wagon rather than an established shop in town, offering their services to the farmers and sharing whatever news they had.

This absence of contact with the outside world makes Benjamin's early achievement—the creation of a clock when he was about 22—all the more astonishing. The achievement also brought him to the attention of his neighbors. They may not have known Banneker the farmer, but they quickly learned about Banneker the clockmaker. People traveled to the farm from considerable distances, simply to see the clock that Benjamin had built.

Banneker the Farmer

On July 10, 1759, Robert Banneky died. Benjamin was 28 years old and now the legal owner of the family farm. His sisters had married and left home, although they all lived in the surrounding community. While Benjamin inherited the larger farm, the three sisters all received a share in Timber Poynt, the first land their parents had ever bought.

As Benjamin began the work of managing the farm with the help of his mother, his grandmother, Molly, died. The specific date of her death, and what became of her farm after her death, is not known.

Benjamin and his mother lived quietly and simply. At some point near or soon after his father's death, the family name was changed in legal documents from Banneky to Banneker. It is not clear why this change was made, but future writings by Benjamin all used the last name Banneker.

Mary Banneker made the clothes she and her son wore. The suit Banneker commonly wore was of plain coloring, woven from linen or cotton. He often wore a tall beaver hat.

At some point, Banneker obtained a flute and a violin, and he taught himself to play them. At the end of the day, when the chores of the farm were completed, he would sit and play softly to himself or to whichever members of his family were visiting.

The rhythms of farm life continued as they had when his father was alive. Banneker continued to raise tobacco for marketing. He cared for his horses and cows. He owned beehives and sold the honey. He raised grain, fruits, and vegetables.

When he was 32, Banneker bought his first book. It was a Bible. Families cherished their Bibles and often noted significant events in them—births, deaths, and marriages of family members, for example. In his Bible, *The Life of Benjamin Banneker* reports, Banneker first wrote: "I bought this book of Honora Buchanan the 4th day of January 1763. B.B." Later, he also noted: "Benjamin Banneker was born November the 9th, in the year of the Lord God, 1731" and "Robert Banneker departed this life July the 10th, 1759."

Banneker continued the family custom of keeping to himself, but his reputation as a clockmaker had brought him to the attention of his neighbors. The fact that he was a learned man began to spread. As Molly Welsh had told him, the skills of reading and writing were precious, and not everyone had them. Gradually, neighbors began to come to ask Banneker to help them with a calculation for their farm, to write a letter, or to read a legal document.

THE ELLICOTT FAMILY

Sometime near 1770, five brothers from Pennsylvania—Joseph, Andrew, Nathaniel, Thomas, and John Ellicott—began exploring the area around the Patapsco River. The brothers had become experts

When the Ellicott brothers arrived in Maryland, they planned on expanding their business of building and repairing gristmills, like the one above.

at building and repairing gristmills (mills used to grind cereals and wheat into flour) for other people. Now, they wanted to use their skills and designs to build new, modern gristmills that they would operate themselves.

The area around the Patapsco River had much to offer. It was about 10 miles (16.1 km) west of Baltimore, which had become the county seat and an area of increasing political and commercial importance. It was also close to several other river towns and seaports from which their flour could be exported.

The brothers purchased 700 acres (283.3 ha), divided into two separate tracts. John and Andrew Ellicott began building the mills in

January 1771, carving a path through the forest from the site of their mills to the river. Then the land had to be cleared for the site. Workmen were brought in. The first gristmill was built and it was impressive in scope. Silvio Bedini states in *The Life of Benjamin Banneker* that the mill was 100 feet (30.5 meters) long, 36 feet (10.9 m) wide, and 1 1/2 stories high, built entirely of stone. There was a wide arch underneath it through which horses and wagons could pass to unload corn, rye, and wheat, which would then be lifted up to the top of the mill to be processed. The Ellicotts also built the first bridge over the Patapsco River to make it easier to transport their flour to market.

These construction projects created great excitement in that isolated community, and 41-year-old Banneker was among those who arrived to study what was being done. He had heard the rumors of gristmills being built but did not believe them at first, since farmers in the region grew far more tobacco than grain. But the construction, less than a mile from his farm, sparked his curiosity.

To add to the construction and chaos, homes were built nearby for members of the Ellicott family, as well as the workers brought from Pennsylvania to complete the project. John Ellicott moved his family into their new home in 1774; Joseph Ellicott's family arrived in 1775. Andrew Ellicott's family arrived far later—in 1797. As the families arrived, they began planting wheat in some of the cleared fields nearby. By the time the mills were ready to start grinding grain into flour, the Ellicotts had their harvest ready and could grind their own wheat into flour and sell it in Baltimore. Neighbors soon followed their example, and they began growing wheat and taking it to the Ellicott mills for grinding.

Gradually, Banneker moved from studying the construction to studying the operating mills. He was intrigued by the mechanics of the operation, by the ways in which machinery lifted the bags of grain into the mill, emptied them, and then carried the ground grain to a loading platform and poured it into barrels. He had seen other mills where corn, rye, and wheat were ground for use by families, but those were much more basic.

Soon, the Ellicotts sought out their neighbor. Many of the workmen were living in a single structure, a kind of boardinghouse, on the grounds of the mill. The long workdays left them little time to plant fields or grow their own food. The Ellicotts needed help feeding their workers, and there was no nearby shop or tavern. Instead, they introduced themselves to Benjamin Banneker and his mother, who were living close by and producing more than enough food. Gradually, arrangements were made so that, each day, 70-year-old Mary Banneker would bring vegetables, eggs, fruit, honey, and poultry or other meat to the boardinghouse to feed the workers.

The Ellicotts were quick to seize opportunities, and once the mills had been completed, they turned their attention to building a country store for the community. The store offered staple food products, tools, and supplies. Eventually, the Ellicotts were able to arrange for regular mail service, and a post office was added to the store. The store soon became a community center where neighboring farmers gathered to pick up their mail, trade or purchase goods, and share news.

Banneker enjoyed traveling to the store, listening to the local gossip and the discussion of politics. He met all of the Ellicotts there, and he gradually formed friendships with them. He admired their goals and what they had accomplished. They were fascinated by his ability to recall details of things he had read, speaking knowledgeably on a wide range of subjects. Banneker became particularly known as an expert on the history of the early settlement of North America and the experiences of the settlers as they established the colonies. It was at the Ellicott & Co. store that Banneker was finally able to regularly read the first newspaper in Baltimore, *The Maryland Journal and Baltimore Advertiser*, which began publication in 1773, and learn of the calls for revolution that were spreading through the colonies.

QUAKER VIEWS ON SLAVERY

The Ellicott family were members of the Society of Friends, also known as Quakers. Quakers were opposed to the notion of slavery and, as the colonies moved toward revolution, argued forcefully that rights and freedoms should be extended to all people, regardless of the color of their skin.

New Jersey Quaker John Woolman (1720–1772) was among those who believed that his faith compelled him to speak out against slavery, as noted in this excerpt from his journal:

> Placing on Men the Ignominious Title, SLAVE, dressing them in uncomely Garments, keeping them to servile Labour, in which they are often dirty, tends gradually to fix a Notion in the Mind, that they are a Sort of People below us in Nature, and leads us to consider them as such in all our Conclusions about them...
>
> Selfishness being indulged, clouds the Understanding; and where selfish Men, for a long Time, proceed on their Way without Opposition, the Deceivableness of Unrighteousness gets so rooted in their Intellects, that a candid Examination of Things relating to Self-interest is prevented; and in this Circumstance, some who would not agree to make a Slave of a Person whose Colour is like their own, appear easy in making Slaves of others of a different Colour, though their Understandings and Morals are equal to the Generality of Men of their own Colour.
>
> The Colour of a Man avails nothing in the Matters of Right and Equity...

[Source: John Woolman, *A Journal of the Life, Gospel Labors, and Christian Experiences of that Faithful Minister of Jesus Christ, John Woolman*, excerpted in Mildred Bain and Ervin Lewis (eds.), *From Freedom to Freedom: African Roots in American Soil* (New York: Random House, 1977), pp. 208–209.]

CHANGES IN THE TIDEWATER

The Ellicotts, by promoting the growth of wheat, were at the forefront of a movement that was slowly sweeping through the Tidewater region of Maryland and Virginia in the period leading up to the American Revolution. In many parts of Maryland and Virginia, farmers were slowly moving away from growing tobacco to growing wheat as their main income crop.

Tobacco was hard on the land, and it required year-round attention. The best tobacco was produced in the first few years of farming a field. Many of the nutrients were leached out of the soil after a few years, and the tobacco became much harsher. Over the years, the price a tobacco crop brought dropped sharply, forcing many tobacco farmers into debt. According to Hamilton Owens in *Baltimore on the Chesapeake*, the tobacco grown in Maryland was not popular in England in the second half of the eighteenth century. It was preferred instead by lower-class smokers in countries like Germany, France, and Holland. In these countries, however, many peasants were learning to grow their own tobacco, and if the price was too high for tobacco imported from Maryland, they would simply smoke their homegrown variety instead. The business of marketing tobacco depended on English ships and English tobacco merchants, and as dissatisfaction with England's rule began to spread throughout the colonies, many farmers chose not to depend for their ability to survive on English merchants. George Washington, in nearby Virginia, was one farmer who had planted great stretches of tobacco but, in 1767, stopped planting the crop and instead switched to selling wheat. While Banneker was impressed by the Ellicotts' mill, he did not immediately abandon growing tobacco in favor of wheat but instead chose to continue to plant the crop that had supplied his family's needs for many years.

At some point shortly before the outbreak of the American Revolution, Mary Banneker died. The exact date is not known; it is believed to have been sometime between 1773 and the middle of 1775. Banneker continued managing the farm, and he also learned how to do the chores his mother had performed. He mastered the art of cooking meals. He did his own washing, cleaning, and mending.

Banneker closely followed the progress of the Revolutionary War through discussions at the Ellicotts' store and in the Baltimore paper, but it had little direct impact on him personally. The Militia Law of 1777 specified that free blacks were not expected to serve in the Continental army. This law was revised in 1790, but three years later, a new law specified that military service was limited to white men.

While some colonies saw multiple battles and served as the site for critical points of the Revolutionary War, this was not the case for Maryland. When British troops had threatened Philadelphia—the home of the Continental Congress—the congress had briefly moved to Baltimore in 1776, but then it returned to Philadelphia. The last royal governor of Maryland, Sir Robert Eden, was popular and, when word of the outbreak of fighting at Lexington and Concord reached Maryland, Eden did not take any dramatic action. Patriots peacefully seized Maryland's military supplies, raised their own colonial troops, and transferred governing authority from Eden to their own revolutionary council. Eden remained in Maryland for some time until finally local patriots politely suggested that he might wish to leave, as they were in the process of preparing for independence. He finally boarded a British warship and peacefully left to return to England.

Troops passed through Baltimore, heading for battles in the north and south, but fighting did not occur near Banneker's home. Some members of the Ellicott family served in the Revolutionary War, several of them being forced to give up their membership in the Society of Friends (whose beliefs included pacifism, or being opposed to war or violence) because of their role in the military. In some cases, this membership was reinstated after the war had ended.

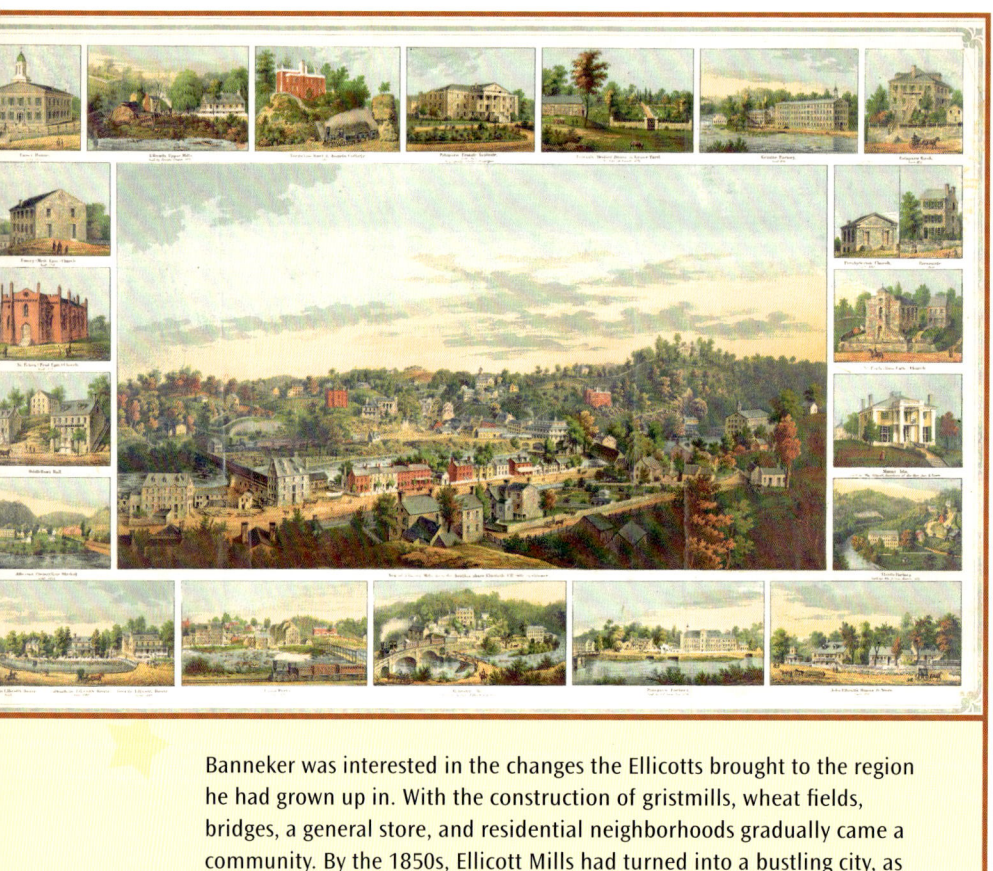

Banneker was interested in the changes the Ellicotts brought to the region he had grown up in. With the construction of gristmills, wheat fields, bridges, a general store, and residential neighborhoods gradually came a community. By the 1850s, Ellicott Mills had turned into a bustling city, as this postcard displays.

With the end of the war, the Ellicotts focused on expanding their businesses. New merchandise was brought into their stores. When word of the arrival of new shipments of goods reached Banneker, he quickly went to the shop, eager to inspect the books, newspapers, and farm tools. The Ellicotts built a school for children in the neighborhood, and they hired qualified teachers to operate it. They built a large warehouse and a wharf in Baltimore to serve in their business of exporting flour to England. Then they decided to build a road for wagons, to run from their mills to Baltimore, and a second road that would connect their mills with Frederick Town, in the opposite direction. One of Andrew Ellicott's sons, George Ellicott, was given the responsibility for surveying the land and laying out both sections of the road.

GEORGE ELLICOTT

George Ellicott had moved with his family to Maryland when he was only 12 years old and from a young age had demonstrated an interest in the sciences and a talent for mechanical work. The road he was surveying would become the major route between the two growing communities.

Benjamin Banneker had met George Ellicott before he began his surveying work, most likely when both men were at the Ellicott store. Because of his interest in building things and in the sciences, George Ellicott had been fascinated by his family's stories of Banneker's clock, and gradually he began to visit Banneker at home to see his clock and discuss their mutual interest in the sciences. The two men became friends, the differences in their race and age (Banneker was 29 years older) no obstacle to their mutual interests in studying how things worked and in English literature. George Ellicott eventually began to lend Banneker his books and surveying instruments. Banneker pored over the texts and experimented with surveying on his own farm.

Banneker had also formed a connection with Joseph Ellicott, one that was based on the clockmaking interest they shared. Joseph Ellicott had built his own watch and clock and owned an impressive collection of timepieces. He also had an array of clockmaker's tools.

One of Joseph Ellicott's proudest accomplishments was a large clock he had built that was nearly eight feet (2.4 m) high. The clock was shaped like a pillar and had four faces, or dials. One face showed the Earth, Moon, and other planets revolving around the Sun. One face showed the hours, minutes, and seconds, plus the days, months, years, and phases of the moon. One face listed 24 musical tunes, one of which was played each hour. There was a pointer on this face that could be moved to a particular tune and the tune would then play. The final face was actually a plate of glass through which you could see the wheels of the clock. Joseph's home had a special place of honor designed to display the clock, and one day he invited Banneker to see the impressive timepiece. Banneker was intrigued and studied the clock carefully.

These connections marked a change in Banneker's life. Previously he had lived a quiet existence, focusing on his farming and spending most of his free time alone or, before her death, with his mother. But now a shop, construction projects, and lively conversation were only a short walk from his home. The arrival of the Ellicotts had brought new social connections to Banneker's life, and soon they would introduce him to a subject that would spark a new interest—the study of astronomy.

5

Studying the Stars

George Ellicott's uncle had encouraged him to study astronomy, and so he ordered several books on the subject to be shipped to the family store. When he had read them, he shared them with Banneker. Next, he ordered a pair of globes—one showing the Earth, the other the stars. He also ordered a special astronomical guide written by George Wright in London, one of the foremost astronomers of the time, as well as a telescope to observe the heavens.

Banneker was fascinated by astronomy, by being able to observe the stars through the telescope, by looking up and identifying the stars he could see in the nighttime sky on Ellicott's globe of the stars. He no longer had the opportunity for many meetings with Ellicott, who married in 1790 and traveled frequently for his family's business, but when they did get together, Ellicott taught

Banneker what he knew about astronomy. On one visit he brought a pedestal telescope and a set of drafting instruments that could be used to make notes on the times of the stars on the meridian and their rising and setting, as well as several books. It was a short visit, and he did not have time to fully train Banneker in the use of the instruments but promised to do so upon his return. He later sent a large, sturdy table for Banneker to use as a work surface for the instruments, more reliable than the somewhat unsteady table Banneker's father had built many years before.

Banneker quickly set to work studying the drafting instruments, removing them from their velvet-lined cases and examining them carefully. He opened the books, filled with complicated text and illustrations. The day slipped away as Banneker attempted to make sense of each book.

He began with James Ferguson's *An Easy Introduction to Astronomy*. It was a fairly straightforward book intended for beginners to the subject, and Banneker easily understood its instructions on the ways to construct projections of eclipses and how to use compasses, rulers, and sectors. Next he pored over a more advanced volume by Ferguson and then studied Charles Leadbetter's *A Compleat System of Astronomy*. One of the books lent by Ellicott was in Latin, accompanied by an English translation.

Banneker read through each book, using the instruments to further study the concepts in the text. He gazed at the stars, making notes about the cycles of the Moon, and then decided to project when an eclipse of the Sun might occur. An eclipse of the Sun—a solar eclipse—takes place when a new moon passes between the Earth and the Sun. The shadow of the Moon falls on the Earth, so that it seems as if the Sun is partially or completely hidden by the Moon. Projecting an eclipse involves drawing the predicted paths of the Sun and Moon while in eclipse.

Studying the Stars 53

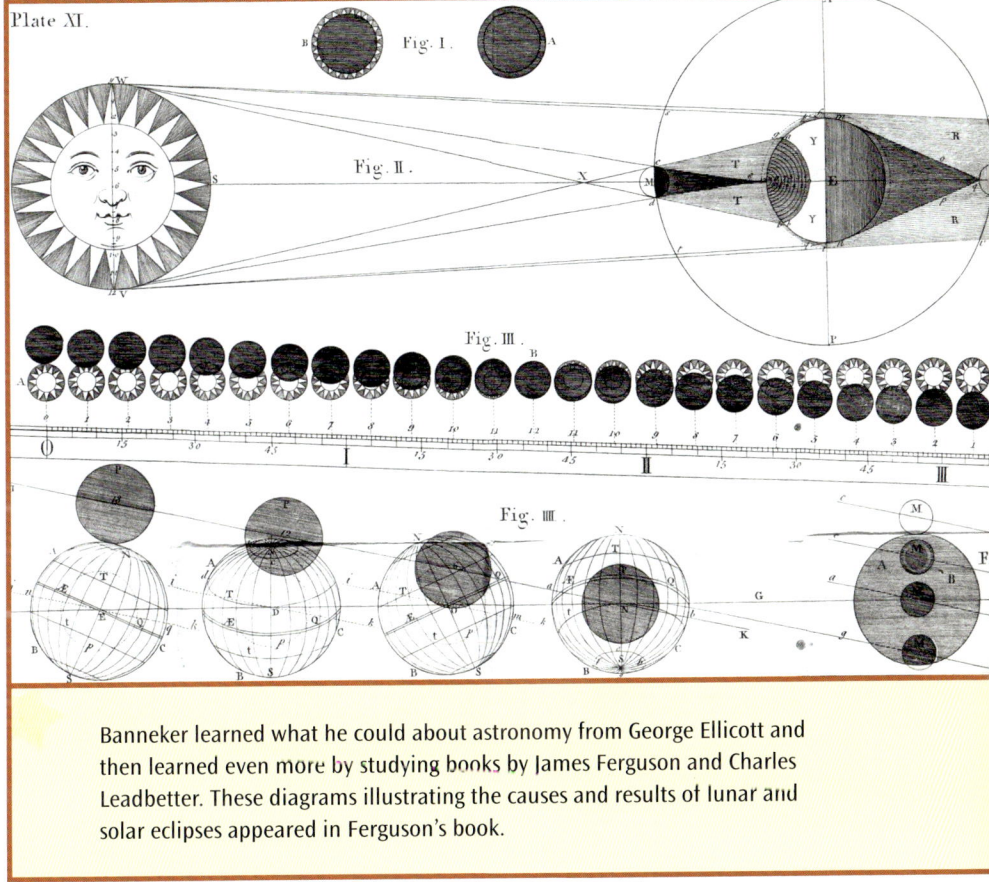

Banneker learned what he could about astronomy from George Ellicott and then learned even more by studying books by James Ferguson and Charles Leadbetter. These diagrams illustrating the causes and results of lunar and solar eclipses appeared in Ferguson's book.

Projecting when a solar eclipse might happen was a complicated procedure, involving advanced mathematics, but Banneker finally succeeded. He wanted to show it to George Ellicott, but Ellicott was away. Finally, Banneker decided to send his friend his projection. Banneker then attempted to focus on his farming, but his mind was constantly filled with his new interest, and after a long day of farming, he would spend many hours each night studying the stars through his borrowed telescope.

Ellicott was astonished when he received Banneker's sketch. He had not had time to explain the instruments or provide any kind of

> ## POOR RICHARD'S ALMANACK
>
> One of the most famous almanac publishers of the eighteenth century was Benjamin Franklin. Franklin published his first almanac in December 1732, calling it *Poor Richard's Almanack*. In addition to the traditional almanac contents—weather forecasts, times of the tide, changes in the Moon—Franklin decided to include jokes, riddles, and poems. It was published annually until 1758, became very popular, and made Franklin a wealthy man.
>
> In the preface to his very first almanac, Franklin introduces humor to explain his reasons for publishing the text:
>
>> I might in this place attempt to gain thy Favour, by declaring that I write Almanacs with other View than that of the publick Good; but in this I should not be sincere; and Men are nowadays too wise to be deceiv'd by pretences.... The plain Truth of the Matter is, I am excessive poor, and my Wife, good Woman, is, I tell her, excessive proud; she cannot bear, she says, to sit spinning ... while I do nothing but gaze at the Stars; and has threatned more than once to burn all my Books and Rattling-Traps (as she calls my Instruments) if I do not make some profitable Use of them for the good of my Family.
>
> [Source: J.A. Leo Lemay, *The Life of Benjamin Franklin, Vol. II: Printer and Publisher, 1730–1747* (Philadelphia: University of Pennsylvania Press, 2006), pp. 174–175.]

introduction to the texts, yet Banneker had obviously fully grasped their content. He discovered a small error in the calculations, made a note of it, then returned it to Banneker, apologizing that business continued to keep him away.

At first Banneker was embarrassed at the mistake. He reviewed his steps, but he could not decide where he had gone wrong. Finally, he turned back to the books he had used to figure out how the error had occurred. He soon discovered that two of the books—written by leading English astronomy experts—contained a disparity, which had led to his error. He wrote to Ellicott, explaining why he had made the mistake and suggesting that, if he continued to study, he might be able to create his own almanac.

CONSIDERING AN ALMANAC

Almanacs were popular reading in the eighteenth century, and nearly every home had one. They generally outsold all other books and pamphlets, and most people purchased one each year. Some almanacs were only a single sheet of paper and provided simply a basic calendar. But the more popular almanacs served as both calendar and datebook for eighteenth-century families. The almanacs listed the times of sunrise and sunset, the phases of the Moon, high and low tides, and eclipses. They contained useful local information—dates of fairs, markets, and other events, distances between points on a particular road, and weather forecasts. Farmers could use this information to determine when they should plant and harvest their crops. Fishermen and sailors used the positions of the stars and Moon to navigate, and they followed the projections of high and low tides. Many eighteenth-century homes did not have clocks—they could use the almanac, with its listings of when sunrise and sunset would take place each day, to estimate time.

Almanacs contained *ephemerides*, astronomical tables that show the calculated positions of the Sun, Moon, and planets for each day of the year. From this, a large amount of important information could be determined, including the expected weather for a day and the time of high and low tides.

Because this varied from region to region, almanacs were published for specific parts of the country. The almanac printed in Maryland would be different from one printed in Massachusetts. Printers found the almanacs to be very profitable, but it was difficult to find trained astronomers to prepare the complicated ephemerides.

Banneker was interested in preparing information for a farmer's almanac, an almanac that focused on issues key to farmers. George Ellicott was initially surprised at Banneker's proposal to prepare an ephemeris for a farmer's almanac, but as he considered the idea, he decided Banneker was certainly capable of making the needed calculations. Then he would simply need to find a printer to publish what he had calculated. He encouraged Banneker to get started.

For several months, in the scarce free time he had when not busy on the farm, Banneker continued his study of the projection of eclipses. He obtained some additional books to help with the calculations, learning new directions and formulas. Finally, he was able to produce all of the needed calculations. Next, he began the process of compiling the needed projections for each month of the coming year.

In *The Life of Benjamin Banneker*, Silvio Bedini quotes from George Ellicott's daughter, Martha, who remembered her mother's description of a visit with friends to Banneker during this time. Banneker's door was wide open, and he was so focused on what he was doing that they came in without him noticing them. Finally spotting them, he stood up and politely asked them to be seated. He was working at the table George Ellicott had given him, and it was covered with astronomy books and scientific equipment. He noted that his passion for astronomy and mathematics was "quite unsuited to a man of his class" and explained that he unfortunately was only making slow progress because he had to spend so much time in the fields running his farm.

Studying the Stars 57

Banneker wanted to use his talents to compile an almanac for farmers. Almanacs were common during that time, but it is the *Poor Richard's Almanack* that is best remembered. Benjamin Franklin (*above*, overseeing printing of his almanac) published the popular almanac and added bits of wisdom and humor to the typical forecasts.

Banneker's calculations were finally completed by the beginning of the spring of 1790. He had predicted the positions of the Sun, Moon, and stars for each month of 1791. He had calculated the weather, and he had made notes for farmers of the best times to plant and harvest their crops. He checked and rechecked his calculations, determined to prevent any errors.

Finally, he copied his calculations into the format used in published almanacs, one sheet for each month. He carefully packed up the sheets and sent them to a printer in Baltimore that published almanacs. His work was rejected. Again he sent it off, and again it was rejected. At last, he sent it to John Hayes, publisher of the *Maryland Gazette* and the man who had published almanacs calculated by another member of the Ellicott family, Andrew Ellicott, a cousin of George Ellicott then living in Philadelphia.

Banneker waited anxiously, but each time that he went to the Ellicott store to collect his mail, there was no word from Hayes. Finally, he wrote to Hayes directly, and he learned that Hayes had sent Banneker's work to Andrew Ellicott to review. Banneker decided to write to Ellicott, asking him for his comments on the work so that Hayes could determine whether or not it was worthy of publication. Banneker also pointed out in his letter that an almanac with his calculations would be of great public interest, as he believed it to be the first in America by "a person of my Complection."

Hayes waited several months before deciding not to publish Banneker's work. The delay was particularly frustrating to Banneker, as it came too late in the year for him to submit the 1791 calculations to another printer. His hard work had all been wasted. Before he could approach another publisher, Banneker would have to complete a new set of calculations for 1792.

By December 1790, Banneker was once more at his table, carefully calculating the positions of the Sun, Moon, and Earth for another year. He was 59 years old. Each day, he rose with the sun, cared for the farm's livestock, made any needed repairs, and checked on the seeds he had put aside for spring. When the sun had set, he once more pulled out his ruler and compass, working well into the night.

A LETTER TO A FRIEND

Banneker did not know that his letter to Andrew Ellicott, written in May 1790, had been forwarded by Ellicott to a man named James Pemberton. Pemberton was one of the leaders (along with Benjamin Franklin) of the Pennsylvania Society for Promoting the Abolition of Slavery, the Relief of Free Negroes Unlawfully Held in Bondage and for Improving the Condition of the African Race, and became its president in 1790. The group had been formed in 1775; many of its members were Quakers.

By 1790, the Pennsylvania Society (as it was more commonly known) was focusing its efforts on developing antislavery movements in other states. Spinoff groups were formed in New York, New Jersey, Rhode Island, Delaware, Virginia, and Maryland. One of their goals was to disprove the belief many Americans held that people of color were inferior to whites.

When Pemberton received the letter forwarded by Andrew Ellicott, he quickly understood how important Banneker's work could be in the Pennsylvania's Society's efforts. He asked the leader of the Maryland Society, a man named Joseph Townsend who was based in Baltimore, to find out everything he could about Banneker.

It did not take long for Townsend to gather the necessary information. One of the members of the Maryland Society was a member of the Ellicott family, George's brother Elias. Another was the printer John Hayes, who had rejected Banneker's work but explained that he had done so not because it was inaccurate but because he already had another almanac to publish.

The two groups—the Pennsylvania Society and the Maryland Society—decided to combine their efforts to ensure that Banneker's work for 1792 would be published. The evidence that a free black man had achieved such complex calculations would be invaluable to their campaign to prove that it was lack of opportunity, rather than lack of ability, that was hindering black Americans.

6

Surveying a New Capital

In 1790, as Benjamin Banneker was attempting to have his almanac calculations published, President George Washington had signed a bill approving the construction of a new capital for the new nation. When Washington was sworn in as the first president of the United States, the capital had been in New York City. Later it was moved to Philadelphia. A provision in the Constitution had called for the Congress to establish a seat of government, but it did not include details of where that should be.

Fierce debate marked the discussion of where the nation's new capital should be located. With so many different states trying to preserve or increase their influence in the new nation, a total of 16 different sites were proposed at various times. In *His Excellency, George*

Washington, Joseph J. Ellis notes that one congressman, frustrated at the intense lobbying, suggested that the new capital should be put on wheels and rolled from one place to another.

James Madison of Virginia was a strong supporter of locating the capital on the Potomac River, not far from his home at Montpelier. Behind-the-scenes negotiations between Madison and Andrew Hamilton, the secretary of the treasury (who needed Madison's support for his economic policy plans), ensured that the Potomac site was the ultimate choice. Finally, in 1790, Congress approved a bill specifying that the site of the new capital would be on the Potomac River. President George Washington, whose Mount Vernon home was nearby, approved the choice. The states of Virginia and Maryland agreed to give up a portion of their territories in exchange for a grant of $200,000. The new capital territory was to be known as the District of Columbia.

On January 24, 1791, George Washington issued a presidential proclamation announcing the planned construction of the new capital and ordering a survey to be made of a 10-mile (16.1 km) square near the Maryland town of Georgetown and the lower falls of the Potomac River, where buildings for the president, Congress, and other government offices were to be built. The vastness of this square had also sparked some controversy. Secretary of State Thomas Jefferson had suggested that the capital be constructed as a small village, which then could expand as needed. But Washington preferred the plans of Pierre Charles L'Enfant, whom he had appointed as chief architect. L'Enfant's vision was for a grand capital, which would be empty at first but gradually fill up with people and offices.

The president had already appointed three commissioners to be in charge of surveying the territory and designing the new city: Daniel Carroll and Thomas Johnson of Maryland and David Stuart of Virginia. The commissioners needed an expert surveyor to define

Surveying a New Capital

Banneker was involved in the surveying of the young nation's new capital, the District of Columbia. Although he was 60 years old, Banneker left his home for the first time and embarked on a project that would greatly excite him.

the area that would become the new capital. They chose Andrew Ellicott. Ellicott had made important connections in the federal government while based in Philadelphia (then the capital). He was a friend of Benjamin Franklin, and Ellicott had been responsible for surveying the boundary between Pennsylvania and Virginia in 1784 and the western boundary of the state of New York from 1789 to 1790.

Ellicott's initial assignment was clear: He was to set the boundaries for the new territory using the points specified by Washington, an area lying between Rock Creek and Goose Creek on the Potomac. From those basic points, he was to construct a 10-mile (16.1 km) square and map the course of the rivers it contained.

Ellicott needed assistants to help him with the project. He had worked before on surveying projects with his two younger brothers, but they were both still busy completing the survey of the western borders of New York State. Next, he contacted his young cousin, George Ellicott, who had proved his surveying skills in the Baltimore-Frederick road project, to see if he might be able to serve as his scientific assistant. But George was busy with his work for the family business. Responsibility for managing the grain mills and several other businesses now belonged to him and his brothers.

George reminded his cousin of Benjamin Banneker, who had the scientific knowledge and the skill with using instruments to make daily observations. Andrew Ellicott recalled the ephemeris he had reviewed and agreed that Banneker might be a good choice. One of his major reservations was Banneker's age. He was 60 years old. The surveying would require long days standing outdoors, in an area that was largely swampland, and nights spent camping outdoors on the site. Finally, he agreed to meet with Banneker and determine whether or not he would want to accept the assignment.

LEAVING THE FARM

Banneker was honored and excited at the proposal Andrew Ellicott offered. He had never been away from home before, but he knew that the challenge of surveying the nation's new capital was a once-in-a-lifetime opportunity. While Ellicott visited with his family in the area, Banneker began making arrangements for his farm to be managed in his absence. Two of Banneker's sisters, who lived nearby, agreed to care for the animals and house until his return.

Before leaving, Banneker met with George Ellicott and the two excitedly discussed how astronomy would be useful in the surveying and what the job would involve. George told Banneker that his cousin Andrew owned some of the finest astronomical instruments in the country, and Banneker would have the opportunity not simply to study them but to use them himself. Silvio Bedini writes in *The Life of Benjamin Banneker* that George Ellicott's wife, Elizabeth, kindly arranged to supply Banneker with a better wardrobe, knowing that he would undoubtedly meet several famous people during the course of his work, possibly even President Washington himself.

The 60-year-old Banneker and the 38-year-old Andrew Ellicott set off on horseback on February 7, 1791. Banneker quickly grew tired. He was not accustomed to riding long distances on horseback, and he was beginning to suffer from the early stages of arthritis. They rode for some time, stopping for a meal and rest before continuing on to Alexandria, in Virginia, where they arrived in a rainstorm and spent the night in a tavern. This was the largest city Banneker had ever seen, far larger than Baltimore at the time. He had time to explore it—the rain continued for several days, making it impossible to do any kind of accurate surveying.

The first surveying site was on the upper end of Hunting Creek near Alexandria. Ellicott had hired several workers to assist them, and the first task was to set up a campsite and clear a path through the woods. Banneker's primary responsibility was to maintain the scientific instruments Ellicott needed for his work. The most important of these was an astronomical clock, which had to be checked often; protected from cold, bumps, or vibrations; and wound daily. The surveyors used the stars to help make their measurements. Each time they observed the stars, they noted the exact time of their observations, checking it on the astronomical clock. Banneker eventually began sleeping in the tent that contained the clock, in order to ensure its safety.

In addition to maintaining the clock and the other instruments, Banneker also was responsible for helping Ellicott with his observations. The surveying of the site involved highly precise measurements. Beginning at Jones Point on the west side of the Potomac, the surveyors needed to mark off a 45-degree angle to the northwest and follow it in a straight line for 10 miles (16.1 km). They then moved from the end point to the northeast for 10 miles, then to the southeast for 10 miles. Each step of the process had to be checked and rechecked, making allowances for uneven ground and other obstacles.

Banneker was responsible for observing and recording stars at specific positions at different times during the night, repeating the observations for several nights. He then checked his data and compared it to published star catalogs. This was used to determine latitude. He confirmed the altitudes of the Sun several times a day to check and correct the astronomical clock.

It was cold in February sleeping in a tent. While Banneker spent most of his time working on site with the instruments, he did accompany Ellicott to a meeting with the commissioners charged by Washington to oversee the project. He was learning more about astronomy through the course of his work, and he became far more skilled in using the complicated instruments Ellicott had brought.

On the rare occasions when he had some free time, Banneker used the advanced instruments for his own calculations. He had not abandoned his hope of publishing an almanac and so had begun the task of making the calculations for 1792.

But there was little time to rest. The busiest time for Banneker was at night, when the critical observations of the stars were made. As the Sun began to rise, Banneker was responsible for briefing Ellicott on all that had happened during the night. Throughout the day, he had to take observations of the Sun with an equal altitude instrument in order to confirm that the astronomical clock was still showing the correct time.

Finally, spring arrived, and in early March, Pierre Charles L'Enfant arrived on the scene. L'Enfant, as architect of the new "Federal City" (as it was now being called), needed to use the information from Ellicott's survey to begin sketching the placement of the various government buildings to be located in the capital, using the details of hills and streams that Ellicott could provide.

Banneker remained with the project until late April 1791. At that point, the preliminary surveying of the 10-mile site had been completed and several of the major points in the city specified. Ellicott's two younger brothers had completed their work in New York and were now available to help with the second phase of the project. In late April, Banneker returned to his farm. According to *African American Lives*, Banneker was paid sixty dollars for his work.

RENEWED DREAMS OF AN ALMANAC

Banneker returned to his work on the farm with mixed feelings. He had enjoyed playing a role in such an important project, had relished working with such fine instruments, and had been well treated by Andrew Ellicott. But camping in the harsh conditions and the constant pressure of being responsible for ensuring the precise accuracy of the astronomical clock had worn on him, and he needed rest.

He also was eager to resume work on a new almanac, using the knowledge and experience he had gained during the surveying project. He developed a new routine for himself, sleeping through most of the day so that he could spend the night studying the stars, projecting eclipses, and completing each month's projections. He bought a large notebook, containing 300 pages, and when each month's calculations were complete and final, he copied them on the right-hand pages of the notebook. The left-hand pages he kept blank, providing space for making notes. Banneker's handwriting was neat and precise, a result of the careful tutoring of his grandmother many years before.

By early June 1791, the calculations were complete. Banneker made two copies and sent one each to printers in Baltimore and Georgetown. Then, considering the activities of the Pennsylvania Society for Promoting the Abolition of Slavery, which had already indicated an interest in his work, he decided that it might make sense to attempt to have his almanac published in Philadelphia, as well. This time he sought out George Ellicott for his advice.

George sent a copy of the almanac to his brother, Elias Ellicott, who was a member of the Pennsylvania Society. Elias knew that Banneker's achievements could prove important to the abolitionist movement. Remembering that James Pemberton had been involved in Banneker's first attempt at an almanac, he wrote to Pemberton, telling him that Banneker had now completed a second almanac, this one for 1792. Pemberton was interested, and a copy was sent to him. In the meantime, a speech in Baltimore would give added prestige to Banneker and make the publication of his almanac more important.

JULY 4 SPEECH

A public meeting was held in Baltimore on July 4, 1791, by the Maryland Society for Promoting the Abolition of Slavery. Prominent Maryland abolitionists as well as curious members of the public gathered to celebrate the nation's independence and listen to a speech by Dr. George Buchanan, a well-known and respected doctor.

Buchanan stood before the public and made a daring speech. In it, he called for an end to slavery and listed the accomplishments of several notable black men and women. He specifically mentioned Ignacio Sancho, the writer; Phillis Wheatley, the poet; and Benjamin Banneker, the "Maryland astronomer." The speech was later published in pamphlet form and distributed throughout the region.

As a result of Dr. Buchanan's speech and the public acknowledgment of Banneker's achievements, Pemberton became even more enthusiastic about publishing Banneker's almanac. First, however, he wanted to verify its accuracy. He sent the calculations to David Rittenhouse, then one of the most noteworthy scientists in America and the newly appointed president of the American Philosophical Society. Rittenhouse checked several of the calculations and confirmed their accuracy, writing quickly to Pemberton (as quoted in *The Life of Benjamin Banneker*) that "I think the papers I herewith return to you a very extraordinary performance, considering the Colour of the Author. . . . Every instance of Genius amongst the Negroes is worthy of attention, because their oppressors seem to lay great stress on their supposed inferior mental abilities."

Pemberton confirmed to Banneker that there was great interest in his almanac, including that of prominent Philadelphia printer Joseph Crukshank. Crukshank was one of the founding members of the Pennsylvania Society for the Abolition of Slavery and had published the first American edition of the poems of Phillis Wheatley in 1786.

Banneker was excited to learn that a third printer was interested in his work. With interest in Georgetown, Baltimore, and Philadelphia, it seemed certain that at least one edition of his almanacs would be published that year. But Banneker was also forced to acknowledge that the interest in his almanacs was not so much because of the

PHILLIS WHEATLEY

In his speech of July 4, 1791, Dr. George Buchanan publicly noted the accomplishments of several black men and women, including Benjamin Banneker. Another of those he noted was Phillis Wheatley.

Wheatley was born in 1753 in Gambia, Africa, and sold into slavery at the age of seven. On July 11, 1761, she was sold to the Wheatley family in Boston, who gave her a new name and taught her to read and write. She became a published poet and was given her freedom in 1773. Among her many famous poems is "To the Right Honourable William, Earl of Dartmouth, His Majesty's Principal Secretary of State for North-America," written in the 1770s, from which the following excerpt is taken:

No more, *America*, in mournful strain
Of wrongs, and grievance unredress'd complain,
No longer shalt thou dread the iron chain,
Which wanton *Tyranny* with lawless hand
Had made, and with it meant t'enslave the land.

Should you, my lord, while you peruse my song,
Wonder from whence my love of *Freedom* sprung,
Whence flow these wishes for the common good,
By feeling hearts alone best understood,
I, young in life, by seeming cruel fate
Was snatch'd from *Afric*'s fancy'd happy seat:
What pangs excruciating must molest,
What sorrows labour in my parent's breast?
Steel'd was that soul and by no misery mov'd

Surveying a New Capital 71

That from a father seiz'd his babe belov'd:
Such, such my case. And can I then but pray
Others may never feel tyrannic sway?. . .

[Source: Excerpted in Herb Boyd, *Autobiography of a People: Three Centuries of African American History Told by Those Who Lived It* (New York: Doubleday, 2000), p. 30.]

accuracy of the calculations as it was due to the race of the man who had prepared them.

WRITING TO JEFFERSON

On August 19, 1791, Benjamin Banneker wrote a letter to Thomas Jefferson, then secretary of state, and enclosed a manuscript copy of his almanac calculations. The letter may have been the idea of one of the prominent abolitionists attempting to publish the almanac, as a way to gain additional attention for Banneker's achievements. Whatever the ultimate motivation, Banneker was careful to begin his letter by detailing the role he had played in surveying the District of Columbia, a project with which Jefferson had also been deeply involved. He drew a comparison between the slavery experienced by blacks in America to that the colonists had experienced under British rule. He wrote:

> Suffer me to recall to your mind that time in which the arms and tyranny of the British crown were exerted with every powerful effort in order to reduce you to a state of servitude; look back, I entreat you, on the variety of dangers to which you were exposed; reflect on that time in which every human aid appeared unavailable, and in which even hope and fortitude wore the aspect of inability to the conflict, and you cannot but be led to a serious and grateful sense of your miraculous and providential preservation.

Banneker's letter gently pointed out to Jefferson the injustice in a country that had so recently fought for its own liberty being content with the enslavement of others. "I suppose that your knowledge of the situation of my brethren, is too extensive to need recital here; neither shall I presume to prescribe methods by which they may be

Surveying a New Capital 73

At the Benjamin Banneker Historical Park and Museum in Maryland, a mannequin of Banneker sits at a desk with a copy of the famous letter he sent to Thomas Jefferson in 1791.

relieved, otherwise than by recommending to you and all others, to wean yourselves from those narrow prejudices which you have imbibed with respect to them . . . thus shall your hearts be enlarged with kindness and benevolence towards them."

Banneker concluded his letter by noting that he enclosed a copy of his calculations for the almanac for the coming year, written in his own hand. Jefferson received the letter and the almanac on August 26 and replied within a few days. He thanked Banneker for the almanac and told him that he had forwarded a copy to his friend, the secretary of the Royal Academy of Sciences at Paris. He also included a note indicating that he too hoped that a system would soon be in place to ensure the improvement in the condition of "our black brethren," without giving specifics about how this could be accomplished. Banneker was very pleased by the letter, and his correspondence to Jefferson and the latter's reply were later published in a pamphlet by a Philadelphia printer and distributed when Banneker's first almanac was published.

7

Almanac Author

As plans to finalize the publication of Banneker's almanac proceeded, Pemberton and some other abolitionists decided that a prominent person should be persuaded to write an introduction to the almanac, in order to help draw attention to it. The person they selected was James McHenry, a Maryland senator who had served in the Continental army first as a medic and later as General Washington's private secretary. McHenry had been a member of the Continental Congress and would later serve as secretary of war to President John Adams. He agreed to write the introduction.

But other problems soon arose. Banneker had submitted his manuscripts with the intention that copies could be published by different printers in different cities. But now the publisher in Baltimore, William Goddard, insisted that his understanding was that he would have exclusive rights to Banneker's work. He had already obtained a copy of McHenry's introduction and announced that he intended to go ahead with the publication.

Banneker was horrified at the situation and worried that he had done something wrong by submitting his almanac to more than one printer. Pemberton reassured him and then handled the delicate negotiations with Goddard, ultimately reaching a compromise so that almanacs could be published in both Baltimore and Philadelphia.

While the almanac ultimately was published under Banneker's name, much of the content had been written by others. Most eighteenth-century almanacs followed this practice: One person calculated the ephemerides and the mathematical data; the printer then added other material that might be of interest: poems, stories, recipes, court dates, local meetings, and a list of members of the Cabinet and Senate.

Banneker's almanac included his ephemeris, as well as his calculations for the dates when eclipses would occur. There were details of the rising and setting of the Sun and the Moon and predictions of the weather. Supplemental material included recipes, poetry, "Remarks on the Swiftness of Time," and essays on such topics as "The Stings of Poverty, Disease and Violence," "On Health," and an essay on curing tree diseases. Perhaps more aptly, the almanac also included an essay "On Negro Slavery, and the Slave Trade."

The almanac was given the impressive title "BENJAMIN BANNEKER'S PENNSYLVANIA, DELAWARE, MARYLAND, AND VIRGINIA ALMANAC AND EPHEMERIS FOR THE YEAR OF OUR LORD, 1792."

McHenry's introduction described Banneker as being "about fifty-nine years of age; he was born in Baltimore County; his father was an African, and his mother the offspring of African parents." It noted that he was a farmer on the land where he had been raised,

James McHenry (above) was selected to write the introduction to Benjamin Banneker's almanac, in order to bring attention to the publication. McHenry had signed the Constitution, and it is for him that Baltimore's Fort McHenry is named.

that he was self-taught in astronomy, and that he had made all of the calculations for the almanac on his own. He cited Banneker as "fresh proof that the powers of the mind are disconnected with the colour of the skin."

Banneker's almanac went on sale at the end of 1791. It was so successful that the first printing quickly sold out, and a second edition was produced. As Dick Russell notes in *Black Genius and the American Experience*, it was the first scientific publication ever written by an African American and became widely circulated along the East Coast of the United States.

The success brought fame and attention to Banneker, although he continued to live quietly on his farm. Travelers now began to come there to meet him and to see his clock and the worktable where he kept his instruments and calculations. He no longer planted tobacco; the physical demands of the labor-intensive crop were becoming too much for him, and his income from the almanacs was sufficient to allow him to focus on astronomy and spend less time in the fields. Instead he kept a small garden where he grew enough food for his own needs, while selling some supplies from his orchard and beehives. He also began to focus on the calculations for an almanac for the following year.

PUBLISHED SCIENTIST

Banneker began his calculations for the 1793 edition of his almanac knowing that he no longer needed to worry about whether or not it would be published. Several printers had expressed an interest in his work, but once more he published with Goddard in Baltimore and selected Joseph Crukshank to publish the Philadelphia edition. The format was essentially the same, but in addition to the new data the 1793 edition included longer stories and essays and a note from the publisher citing the success the previous year's edition had enjoyed. It stated that the work had been presented in the British House of Commons as proof for the need to bring an end to the slave trade in Africa. It also included an essay titled "A Plan of a Peace Office for

BANNEKER'S FIRST ALMANAC

The first almanac was published in late 1791. In addition to an introductory letter from James McHenry, it also contained a preface designed to highlight its importance to the abolitionist movement:

> The Editors of the PENNSYLVANIA, DELAWARE, MARYLAND, AND VIRGINIA ALMANACK, feel themselves gratified in the Opportunity of presenting to the Public, through the Medium of their Press, what must be considered an extraordinary Effort of Genius—a COMPLETE and ACCURATE EPHEMERIS for the Year 1792, calculated by a sable Descendant of Africa, who, by this Specimen of Ingenuity, evinces, to Demonstration, that mental Powers and Endowments are not the exclusive Excellence of white People, but that the Rays of Science may alike illumine the Minds of Men of every Clime, (however they may differ in the Colour of their Skin) particularly those whom Tyrant-Custom hath too long taught us to depreciate as a Race inferior in intellectual Capacity—They flatter themselves that a philanthropic Public, in this enlightened Era, will be induced to give their Patronage and Support to this Work, not only on Account of its intrinsic Merit, (it having met the Approbation of several of the most distinguished Astronomers in America, particularly the celebrated Mr. Rittenhouse) but from similar Motives to those which induced the Editors to give this Calculation the Preference, the ardent Desire of drawing modest Merit from Obscurity, and controverting the long-established illiberal Prejudice against the Blacks.

[Source: Silvio A. Bedini, *The Life of Benjamin Banneker* (New York: Scribner's, 1972), pp. 177–178.]

the United States." No author for the essay—which proposed that the U.S. Cabinet should include a Secretary of Peace as well as a Secretary of War—was listed in the original edition. It was later proved to be the work of Benjamin Rush, a well-known Quaker doctor.

The second edition included Banneker's letter to Jefferson and Jefferson's reply. The Philadelphia edition also included material specifically focusing on the abolitionist movement.

Visitors frequently traveled the 10 miles (16.1 km) by horseback from Baltimore to visit Banneker and meet the self-taught mathematician, astronomer, surveyor, and almanac writer. Dick Russell in *Black Genius and the American Experience* notes that Banneker was remembered by one who visited him during this time as being "very precise in conversation and exhibited deep reflection. He seemed to be acquainted with everything of importance that was passing in the country. . . . His head was covered with a thick suit of white hair, which gave him a very venerable and dignified appearance. His dress was uniformly of super fine drab broad cloth, made in the old style of a plain coat, with straight collar and long waistcoat, and a broad-brimmed hat."

The publishers quickly began to pressure Banneker to begin work on an almanac for 1794. A bout of sickness delayed his start on the new project, and his efforts were further complicated by his plan to calculate an ephemerides for an almanac to be published in England. Interest in Banneker had been growing ever since portions of his almanac had been read in the House of Commons as a way to build support for British antislavery activities. Banneker attempted to answer this British interest in his research by beginning calculations for the area around London.

It was yet another ambitious project for the scientist, particularly while battling illness. Ultimately it proved too much for him, and the British calculations were never completed. Instead, Banneker focused what energy he had on preparations for the American

The title page to the 1795 edition of Banneker's almanac. This was the first edition to feature a portrait of the author. By now, his fame had spread.

edition, and the popularity of the 1794 edition was even greater than that of previous editions.

Banneker's fame led to an even wider distribution of the 1795 edition of his almanac. There were at least nine editions of this almanac published, resulting in greater attention—and income—to Banneker. The 1795 edition included, for the first time, a portrait of him on the cover of several of the editions. In one edition—the edition published in Baltimore—he is shown wearing typical Quaker clothing (Banneker had attended several Quaker worship services but never formally joined the Society of Friends or any religious group). In addition to different covers, each publisher chose to supplement his edition with content of specific interest to each region. For example, the Philadelphia edition of the 1795 almanac included a report on the outbreak of yellow fever in that city.

The 1795 edition, as noted in *Black Genius and the American Experience*, included a quote from Banneker: "The most sensible of those who make scientific researches, is he who believes himself the farthest from the goal, & who whatever advances he has made in his road, studies as if he yet knew nothing and marches as if he were only yet beginning to make his first advance."

SLOWING SALES

The 1796 edition of Banneker's almanac did not sell as well as previous editions. Each edition of the almanacs traditionally opened with an introduction that offered the contents as support of the antislavery movement. For example, the 1796 edition included a preface that stated, according to Silvio Bedini, "Although the God of Nature has marked the face of the African with a darker shade than his brethren, he has given him a soul equally capable of refinement."

The 1797 almanac was the last edition that Banneker published, although he continued to calculate ephemerides for the next few years, through 1802. Public support for the antislavery movement was no longer as strong as it had once been. In fact, the Maryland Society for Promoting the Abolition of Slavery closed in 1797, shortly after the final edition of Banneker's almanac was published.

As the eighteenth century drew to a close, the memories of the War for Independence, and the colonists' own struggles against injustice, had begun to fade. National attention was increasingly focused on the problems of building a new nation, of the struggles of President John Adams to direct the republic, of foreign nations like France and Britain still attempting to influence events in the United States. The question of slavery would simmer below the surface for several decades.

Banneker's own health problems also had increased, making the demands of producing an almanac more challenging. He struggled with headaches, and his hands had begun to shake.

It became more difficult for him to perform the daily tasks necessary to farm his land. Finally, noticing that much of his land was no longer being used, neighbors came to Banneker and asked him to rent his land to farm. Banneker agreed, but he proved to be an unsuccessful landlord. He often forgot to collect the rent; on other occasions, his tenants refused to pay him.

His poor health and age made him more of a target, and in later years, neighbors threatened him with violence whenever he attempted to collect what he was owed. Banneker heard suspicious gunfire near his door or would suddenly notice that a coat or horse was missing. His house was broken into (although his valuable scientific instruments and notebooks were not taken). His orchards were stripped of all their fruit.

Finally, Banneker decided to sell his land. It was a difficult and painful decision. His father had worked and sacrificed for years to buy the farmland, and he had specifically placed Benjamin's name on the deed to ensure that the land would belong, without question, to his son upon his death. He had impressed upon Benjamin the importance of the land and how it represented freedom to those who had once suffered as slaves.

But Banneker recognized that he could no longer farm the land himself nor trust his tenants to pay him for its use. The farm amounted to more than 100 acres (40.5 ha).

The Ellicott family had once expressed an interest in buying the land if Banneker ever decided to sell it. When he approached them again, they quickly agreed.

The Ellicotts generously agreed to buy the land while giving Banneker the right to live there for the rest of his life. As part of the arrangement, the Ellicotts agreed to pay Banneker for the land in yearly payments, so that he would have a steady source of income. The Ellicotts purchased 72 of the acres (29.1 ha); Banneker divided the remaining land into 5 smaller plots, which he sold over the next several years when he wanted to add to his income.

In 1799, the arrangement between Banneker and the Ellicotts was changed. He was given a charge account at their store. At the end of the year, the value of the items he had purchased was calculated, deducted from the annual payment due to him, and he was paid the remaining sum in cash. This may have been because Banneker was concerned about the threats and robberies he had experienced and reluctant to keep larger sums of cash in his home. Banneker kept a notebook listing the items he purchased each year, as well as his calculations for eclipses and records of observations and notes about dreams or quotes that appealed to him. The notebooks show that Banneker purchased such items as pork, corn, molasses, cloth, gunpowder, books, and candles, as well as two pairs of shoes each year.

These notebooks also show that in May of 1796 he made one of the most significant purchases of his life. At the age of 64, more than four decades after he had built his famous clock, Benjamin Banneker bought a pocket watch.

8

Final Years

In his final years, Banneker at last had the income and freedom to focus on scientific study. He kept a small garden and tended the trees in his orchard, growing enough fruit and vegetables for his own use.

But most of his time was now focused on observing the world around him. He often spent evenings studying the stars through his telescope or wrapped in a coat and stretched out on the ground, gazing up at the nighttime sky. He went to bed as the sun came up, sleeping for most of the morning and then waking up in the middle of the afternoon. He made extensive notes on the habits of the bees that populated his beehives, as well as what he described as "locusts" (now known as cicadas). He once more enjoyed taking walks around his property, studying and enjoying nature, just as he had done as a boy, and hunting small game.

Late in the day, as the sun began to set, he would play either his flute or his violin. On warm nights he would sit under a chestnut tree near his doorway as he enjoyed the music.

Banneker retained his great interest in mathematical puzzles. He would occasionally bring one that he had created to the Ellicott store and leave it for George Ellicott to solve, and the Ellicotts would leave puzzles that they discovered during their travels at the store for Banneker to collect when he came in for purchases.

As he aged, it became more difficult for Banneker to travel by horseback, even the relatively short distance to the Ellicott store. A young boy, the grandson of Jacob Hall—Banneker's old friend from school—came often to check on Banneker, running errands for him, delivering packages, and carrying messages, even helping to milk Banneker's cow.

The Life of Benjamin Banneker reports that Banneker continued to cook for himself late in life, but they were relatively simple meals. He purchased a large quantity of salt pork from the Ellicotts' store and often boiled it with some corn dumplings and whatever vegetables might be in season in his garden. He did not drink tea or coffee, only milk from his cow.

SLOWING STEPS

Gradually, it became more difficult for Banneker to spend each night outside, studying the stars. His journals show that he maintained his nightly astronomical observations through 1803 and into January 1804. After this, his observations are recorded more randomly, and an ephemeris for 1805 was never completed.

Walking was still a source of pleasure for Banneker, although his steps were slower. On October 9, 1806, he set out for his customary walk, meeting someone he knew and stopping to talk. In the middle of the conversation, Banneker told the acquaintance that he did not

BANNEKER'S OBITUARY

Shortly after Benjamin Banneker's death, the *Federal Gazette* published an obituary of the famous scientist. It shows that in a state where slavery was still widespread, Banneker's accomplishments were recognized and applauded:

> On Sunday, the 9th instant, departed his life at his residence in Baltimore county, in the 73rd [sic] year of his age, Mr. BENJAMIN BANNEKER, a black man, and immediate descendant of an African father. He was well known in his neighborhood for his quiet and peaceable demeanor, and among scientific men as an astronomer and mathematician. In early life he was instructed in the most common rules of arithmetic, and thereafter, with the assistance of different authors, he was enabled to acquire a perfect knowledge of all the higher branches of learning. Mr. B was the calculator of several almanacs which were published in this, as well as some of the neighboring states, and although of late years none of his almanacs were published, yet he never failed to calculate one every year, and left them among his papers, preferring solitude to mixing with society, and devoted the greatest part of his time in reading and contemplation, and to no books was he more attached than the scriptures. At his decease he bequeathed all his astronomical and philosophical books and paper to a friend.
>
> Mr. Banneker is a prominent instance to prove that a descendant of Africa is susceptible of as great mental improvement and deep knowledge into the mysteries of nature as that of any other nation.

[Source: Quoted in Silvio Bedini, *The Life of Benjamin Banneker* (New York: Scribner's, 1972), p. 271.]

feel well, and they walked together back to his house. Banneker lay down and died soon after. He was nearly 75 years old.

Before his death, Banneker had told his relatives that there were certain items that he wanted to give to George Ellicott upon his death. These included the table Ellicott had given him when he first began his studies of astronomy, his precious scientific instruments, and his collection of books on astronomy and surveying. Many of these were items Ellicott himself had given to Banneker; now they were returned. In addition, Banneker had requested that George Ellicott be given his journals, which contained his notes and astronomical calculations, and his copies of his correspondence with Thomas Jefferson. The rest of his possessions were to be divided between his two surviving sisters, Minta and Molly.

Banneker was buried two days later in a grave near his home. As his funeral service was under way, those in attendance noticed that his house was on fire. The simple wooden structure burned quickly, and it was gone before the flames could be extinguished. The contents of the home—those items that had not immediately been removed and given to George Ellicott—were all destroyed, including Banneker's famous clock, which had still been working at the time of his death.

FORGOTTEN PIONEER

For many years after his death, little attention was paid to Banneker or his accomplishments. It was not until the 1840s, as the abolitionist movement again began to gain support throughout the United States, that attention returned to Banneker.

In 1845, a small group, led by Reverend Daniel Alexander Payne of the Bethel Church of the African Methodist Church of Baltimore, set out to explore the area where Banneker had lived to see if they could locate his grave. Payne had delivered a lecture about Banneker's life and work earlier in the year, hoping to inspire young men in his church to study science. Payne and the three other men (representatives from his church) were interested in erecting a monument on the site, and they had already begun raising funds for that purpose.

A local farmer was able to lead them across the land that had once been the Banneker farm. They found the spot where Banneker was buried at last, beneath two tulip trees growing close together. A short distance away, they could see a shallow cavity, marking the spot where Banneker's home had once stood.

Sadly, Payne failed in his effort to raise enough funds for a monument. A prominent Baltimore architect did design a marker for the grave site, in the shape of an Egyptian obelisk, but it was never erected.

Finally, in 1954, just as the civil-rights movement was blossoming, the State Roads Commission of Maryland erected a marker at the spot that historical records suggest was where the Banneker farm had been. It was no longer farmland—instead, it was the site of the Westchester Grade School. The marker read:

BENJAMIN BANNEKER
1731–1806
SELF-EDUCATED NEGRO
MATHEMATICIAN—ASTRONOMER
HE MADE THE FIRST MARYLAND ALMANAC IN 1792.
ASSISTED IN SURVEY OF DISTRICT OF COLUMBIA.
HIS ACHIEVEMENTS RECOGNIZED
BY THOMAS JEFFERSON.
WAS BORN, LIVED HIS ENTIRE LIFE AND
DIED NEAR HERE.

Tragically, the marker was vandalized and stolen several times. In 1969, after efforts to install a sturdier aluminum plaque proved

90 BENJAMIN BANNEKER

Although Benjamin Banneker is not mentioned as often as some of the nation's great historical figures, his contributions to colonial America were significant. History has not forgotten Banneker entirely, however. This portrait was used on a 1980 U.S. postal stamp commemorating Banneker.

useless when the plaque was broken and removed, the State Roads Commission chose to leave the site unmarked. Efforts are now underway to raise funds for a permanent memorial for Banneker.

HIS LEGACY

Benjamin Banneker's life story is filled with extraordinary accomplishments. With little formal education, on an isolated family farm, he taught himself mathematics, astronomy, and surveying. At a young age, he built a clock that continued to keep accurate time for more than four decades. He participated in surveying the site of the new capital of the United States and published several popular and acclaimed almanacs based on his observations of the stars and predictions of tides and weather. He corresponded with Thomas Jefferson, sharing his hope that Jefferson would change his position on slavery.

All of these would have been exceptional accomplishments, but they are made more extraordinary because of who Banneker was and the times in which he lived. Banneker was a free black in a country where far more people of color were enslaved than free. His father and grandfather had both been slaves.

His life was marked by a period of fame, and yet he lived his life quietly, spending most of his adult years on his family's farm. Even today, he is less well known than many other scientists of his time.

Banneker's influence began during his lifetime. His accomplishments were frequently cited as important evidence proving that skin color was no prediction of intelligence or ability. Abolitionists in the eighteenth and nineteenth centuries would use Banneker's success to draw attention to their antislavery activities.

Words from Banneker's Almanac of 1794 (quoted in *Black Genius and the American Experience*) reflect the modest scientist's lifelong personal philosophy: "Presumption should never make us neglect that which appears easy to us, nor despair make us lose courage at the sight of difficulties."

Chronology

1731   Benjamin Banneker is born on November 9.

1753   When Banneker is about 22 (the exact date is not known), he builds a working clock.

1759   Banneker's father dies on July 10, and he inherits the family farm.

TIMELINE

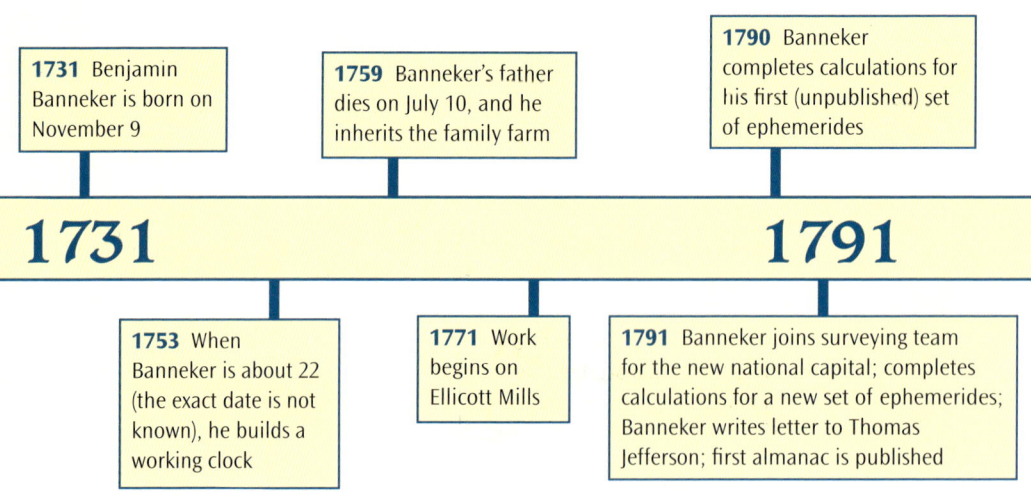

Year	Event
1771	Work begins on Ellicott Mills.
1790	Banneker completes calculations for his first (unpublished) set of ephemerides.
1791	Banneker joins surveying team for the new national capital. Completes calculations for a new set of ephemerides. Banneker writes letter to Thomas Jefferson. First almanac is published.
1792	Second almanac is published.
1793	Banneker attempts work on British almanac; illness forces him to abandon plan. Sales of third edition of almanac exceed previous two years.

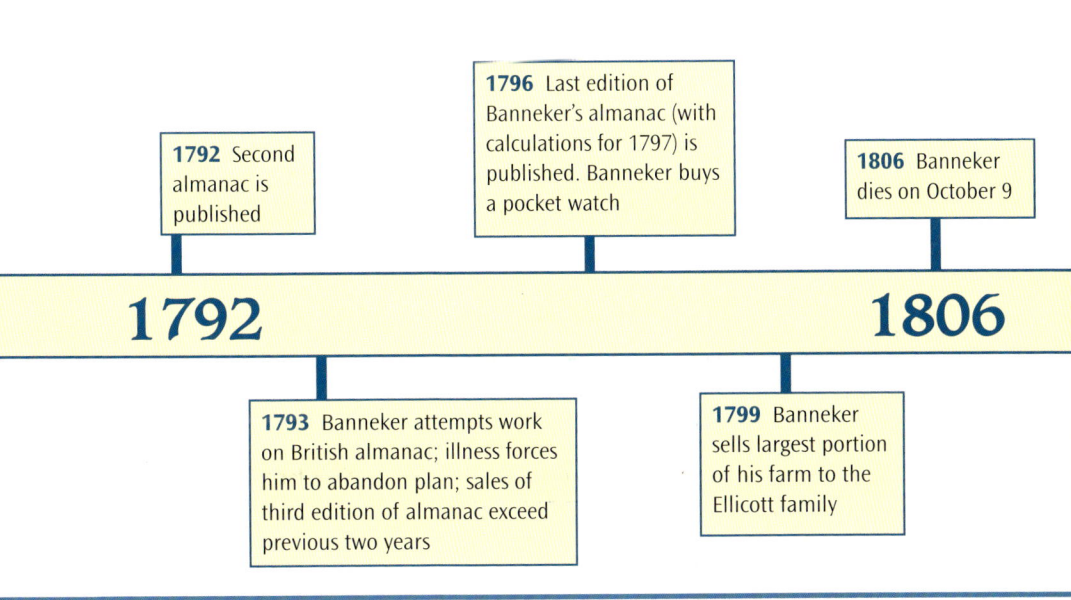

1792 Second almanac is published

1796 Last edition of Banneker's almanac (with calculations for 1797) is published. Banneker buys a pocket watch

1806 Banneker dies on October 9

1793 Banneker attempts work on British almanac; illness forces him to abandon plan; sales of third edition of almanac exceed previous two years

1799 Banneker sells largest portion of his farm to the Ellicott family

1796 Last edition of Banneker's almanac (with calculations for 1797) is published. Banneker buys a pocket watch.

1799 Banneker sells largest portion of his farm to the Ellicott family.

1806 Banneker dies on October 9.

Bibliography

Alden, John Richard. *A History of the South, Vol. III: The South in the Revolution, 1763–1789*. Baton Rouge: La.: Louisiana State University Press, 1957.

Bain, Mildred, and Ervin Lewis, eds. *From Freedom to Freedom: African Roots in American Soil*. New York: Random House, 1977.

Bedini, Silvio A. *The Life of Benjamin Banneker*. New York: Charles Scribner's Sons, 1972.

Berry, Mary Frances, and John W. Blassingame. *Long Memory: The Black Experience in America*. New York: Oxford University Press, 1982.

Brawley, Benjamin. *Early Negro American Writers*. Freeport, N.Y.: Books for Libraries Press, 1968.

Breen, T.H. *Tobacco Culture*. Princeton, N.J.: Princeton University Press, 1985.

Cerami, Charles. *Benjamin Banneker: Surveyor, Astronomer, Publisher, Patriot*. New York: Wiley, 2002.

Conniff, Michael L., and Thomas J. Davis. *Africans in the Americas: A History of the Black Diaspora*. New York: St. Martin's Press, 1994.

Ellis, Joseph J. *His Excellency: George Washington*. New York: Alfred A. Knopf, 2004.

Gates, Henry Louis Jr., and Evelyn Brooks Higginbotham, eds. *African American Lives*. New York: Oxford University Press, 2004.

Gutheim, Frederick. *The Potomac*. New York: Rinehart & Co., 1949.

Hinman, Bonnie. *Benjamin Banneker*. Philadelphia: Chelsea House Publishers, 2000.

Horton, James Oliver. *Free People of Color: Inside the African American Community.* Washington, D.C.: Smithsonian Institution Press, 1993.

Lemay, J.A. Leo. *The Life of Benjamin Franklin, Volume II: Printer and Publishers, 1730–1747.* Philadelphia: University of Pennsylvania Press, 2006.

Litwin, Laura. *Benjamin Banneker.* Berkeley Heights, N.J.: Enslow Publishers, 1999.

Morgan, Philip D. *Slave Counterpoint: Black Culture in the Eighteenth-century Chesapeake & Lowcountry.* Chapel Hill, N.C.: University of North Carolina Press, 1998.

Mullane, Dierdre, ed. *Crossing the Danger Water: Three Hundred Years of African-American Writing.* New York: Anchor Books, 1993.

Owens, Hamilton. *Baltimore on the Chesapeake.* Garden City, N.Y.: Doubleday, Doran & Co., 1941.

Patterson, Lillie. *Benjamin Banneker.* Nashville, Tenn.: Parthenon Press, 1978.

Reiss, Oscar. *Blacks in Colonial America.* Jefferson, N.C.: McFarland & Co., 1997.

Russell, Dick. *Black Genius and the American Experience.* New York: Carroll & Graf, 1998.

Skaggs, David Curtis. *Roots of Maryland Democracy: 1753–1776.* Westport, Conn.: Greenwood Press, 1973.

WEB SITES

Benjamin Banneker Memorial
www.bannekermemorial.org/history

Free Africans Americans of Virginia, North Carolina, South Carolina, Maryland and Delaware
www.freeafricanamericans.com

Further Resources

Cox, Clinton. *Come All You Brave Soldiers: Blacks in the Revolutionary War*. New York: Scholastic Press, 1999.

Fleming, Candace. *Ben Franklin's Almanac*. New York: Atheneum, 2003.

Lester, Julius. *To Be a Slave*. New York: Puffin Books, 1998.

McKissack, Patricia C., and Frederick L. McKissack. *Rebels Against Slavery*. New York: Scholastic, 1996.

Newman, Richard, and Marcia Sawyer. *Everybody Say Freedom: Everything You Need to Know About African-American History*. New York: Plume, 1996.

WEB SITES

***Astronomy* Magazine**
http://www.astronomy.com/asy/default.aspx?c=ss&id=127

Benjamin Banneker Memorial
www.bannekermemorial.org/history.htm

Colonial Williamsburg's "African American Experience"
http://www.history.org/Almanack/people/african

PBS's "Africans in America"
www.pbs.org/wgbh/aia/

University of North Carolina "Documenting the American South"
http:docsouth.unc.edu/neh/

Picture Credits

PAGE

9: Getty Images
14: North Wind Pictures
22: The Print Collector
27: Henry London's free papers, Port Royal, SC, 22 August 1862 (pen and ink on paper), American School (19th century)/Private Collection/Courtesy of Swann Auction Galleries/The Bridgeman Art Library International
32: North Wind Pictures
37: North Wind Pictures
42: Richard T. Nowitz
48: Library of Congress, Prints and Photographs Division, LC-DIG-pga-02596
53: The Print Collector
57: Benjamin Franklin Overseeing the Printing of Poor Richard's Almanack (oil on canvas), Rockwell, Norman (1894–1978)/Private Collection / Lawrence Steigrad Fine Arts, New York/The Bridgeman Art Library
63: North Wind Pictures
71: Library of Congress, Prints and Photographs Division, LC-USZC4-5316
73: Michael Ventura/Alamy
77: Library of Congress, Prints and Photographs Division, LC-USZ62-54696
80: Bettmann/Corbis
90: History/Alamy

Index

Page numbers in *italics* indicate photos or illustrations.

A

abolition 69, 79, 82–83
Adams, John 75
almanacs
   Benjamin Franklin and 54, *57*
   completion of 68
   interest in writing 55–60
   publication of Banneker's first 74, 75–80
   publication of subsequent 80–83, *81*
Atlantic Ocean, crossing of 18

B

Banneky (Banneker), Jemima (sister) 31
Banneky (Banneker), Mary (mother)
   after death of Robert Banneky 25–28
   birth of 24
   death of 46–47
   food sales and 44
Banneky (Banneker), Minta (sister) 31
Banneky (Banneker), Molly (sister) 31
Banneky, Benjamin (grandfather) 22–24, 25
Banneky, Molly (grandmother)
   death of 40
   Elkridge Landing incident and 33–36
   as forced laborer 17–20
   freedom of 20–21
   marriage of to Benjamin Banneky 23–24
   purchase of slaves by 21–23, *22*
Banneky, Robert (father) 25–28, 40
Bibles *32*, 32, 40
birth of Benjamin Banneky 25, 40
British almanac 80
Buchanan, George 69, 70

C

calling for the book 17–18
Calvert, Leonard 36
capital, construction of new 61–67, *63*
Carroll, Daniel 62
Certificates of Freedom *27*, 29
Christianity 23
clocks
   almanacs and 55–60
   building of 15–16, 39, 49
   destruction of 88
   interest in 50, 51–55, *53*
   surveying and 66
A Compleat System of Astronomy (Leadbetter) 52
Continental Congress 47
convicts 18–19
cowpenning 12, 38
Crukshank, Joseph 69, 78
curing 37

99

D

death of Benjamin Banneker 88
Declaration of Independence 10–11, 72–74
discrimination 10–11, 29, 72–74. *See also* Prejudice

E

An Easy Introduction to Astronomy (Ferguson) 52, *53*
eclipses 52, *53*, 56
Eden, Robert 47
education 31–33, 48
Elkridge Landing incident 33–36
Ellicott, Andrew 41–43, 59, 64
Ellicott, Elias 59, 68
Ellicott, George
   almanacs and 56, 68
   astronomy and 51, 53–54
   friendship with 49–50
   items left to after death of Banneker 88
   puzzles and 86
   surveying job and 65
Ellicott, John 41–43
Ellicott, Joseph 41–42, 43, 49–50
Ellicott, Nathaniel 41–42
Ellicott, Thomas 41–42
Ellicott Mills 47–49, *48*
ephemerides 55–56, 76, 80, 82
Equiano, Olaudah 34–35
essays 78–80

F

Federal Gazette obituary 87
felons 18–19
Ferguson, James 52, *53*
forced laborers 19–20
Franklin, Benjamin 54, *57*, 64
freedom 20–21, 29, 34

G

globes 51

Goddard, William 75–76, 78
gristmills *42*, 42–44

H

Hall, Jacob 33, 86
Hamilton, Alexander 62
hangings 17
Hayes, John 58, 59–60
health problems 83
herbs, healing and 31
hogsheads 9–10, 37
hominy 31
honey 31
house, description of 30–31, *32*

I

indentured servants 19–20

J

Jefferson, Thomas, letter to 10–11, 72–74, *73*, 80
Johnson, Thomas 62
Joppa 25
July 4 speech 68–69, 70

L

land ownership 26–28, 83–84
Leadbetter, Charles 52
legacy of Benjamin Banneker 91
L'Enfant, Pierre Charles 62, 67
Levi, Josef 15
London, Henry *27*
London almanac 80
lunar eclipses 53

M

Madison, James 62
mail service 44
manure, cowpenning and 12
marriage, interracial 23–24
Maryland Society 59–60, 68–69, 83
math 33
McHenry, James 75–76, *77*

Militia Law of 1777 47
milk, theft of 17
mills *42*, 42–44
monuments 89

N

name change 40
newspapers 38, 44
Nigeria 34

O

obituary 87

P

pacifism 47
Payne, Daniel Alexander 88–89
Pemberton, James 59, 68–69, 75–76
Pennsylvania Society 59–60, 68, 69
"A Plan of a Peace Office for the United States" 78–80
Poor Richard's Almanack 54, *57*
post office 44
postage stamps *90*
prejudice 28–29. *See also* Discrimination
puzzles and 86

Q

Quakers
  Banneker and 82
  Pennsylvania Society and 59
  Revolutionary War and 47
  on slavery 45

R

reading 17–18, 31–32, 40, 70
Revolutionary War 47
Rittenhouse, David 69
rolling roads 10–11, 21, 25
Rush, Benjamin 80

S

Sancho, Ignacio 69
schooling 31–33, 48
seven years passengers 19
slavery
  auctions and 21–23, *22*
  horrors of 34–35
  Maryland Society on 68–69
  Pennsylvania Society and 59–60
  Quakers on 45
Society of Friends (Quakers)
  Banneker and 82
  Pennsylvania Society and 59
  Revolutionary War and 47
  on slavery 45
solar eclipses 52, *53*
stamps *90*
stealing 17, 20
store, construction of 44
Stuart, David 62
surveying 49–50, 63, 64–67

T

telescopes 51–52
theft 17, 20
Timber Poynt 26, 40
tobacco
  importance of to Banneky family 7–12, *9*, 28, 36–39, *37*
  problems of as crop 46
  slavery and 28–29
tobacco notes 12, 38
Townshend, Joseph 59

W

Washington, George 46, 61–62
watches 13–16, 84
Welsh, Molly. *See* Banneky, Molly
wheat *42*, 42–44, 46
Wheatley, Phyllis 69, 70–71, *71*
Woolman, John 45
Wright, George 51

About the Author

Heather Lehr Wagner is a writer and editor. She is the author of numerous books exploring political and social issues, including several books focusing on the people who shaped colonial America. She is also the author of *William Bradford* in the LEADERS OF THE COLONIAL ERA series.

Heather Lehr Wagner earned a B.A. in political science from Duke University and an M.A. in government from the College of William and Mary. She lives with her family in Pennsylvania.